LIVING WITH
CARPETS

LIVING WITH
CARPETS

A comprehensive, style-by-style directory to choosing

the right carpet for your home

BARTY PHILLIPS

Thames and Hudson

A QUARTO BOOK

First published in Great Britain in 1997
by Thames and Hudson Ltd, London

A catalogue record for this book is
available from the British Library

ISBN 0-500-01812-X

This book was designed and produced by
Quarto Publishing plc
The Old Brewery
6 Blundell Street
London N7 9BH

Senior editor Michelle Pickering
Senior art editors Anne Fisher
and Catherine Shearman
Copy editor Jane Donovan
Designer Roger Daniels
Illustrator Valerie Hill
Map illustrations Arcadia Editions
Photographers Martin Norris
and Les Wies
Picture researchers Zoe Holtermann
and Christine Lalla
Editorial director Pippa Rubinstein
Art director Moira Clinch

Typeset in Great Britain by
Central Southern Typesetters, Eastbourne
Manufactured in Singapore by
United Graphics (Pte) Ltd
Printed in Singapore by
Star Standard Industries Pte Ltd

CONTENTS

A HISTORY OF CARPET STYLES

The most distinctive hand-knotted or woven oriental carpets and rugs that you can buy today are still based on the great weaving traditions of the past. Many traditional and classic designs from all over the world are available, either on the second-hand and antique market, as tribal, village or factory-made continuations of the tradition, or as adaptations and reproductions. They are joined by a variety of modern styles, created by artists and designers for individual or workshop manufacture, either in the West or on village looms in the East. In general, carpets and rugs are basically the same thing, though the word rug is usually taken to mean a smaller object.

KNOTTED-PILE CARPETS

Luxurious oriental carpets and rugs, using the knotted-pile technique, are made in a vast area stretching from Turkey and Iran (Persia) right across the Caucasus to India and China. Knotted-pile carpets are made with short lengths of yarn (usually wool, but sometimes silk) that are looped or knotted round the warp threads on the loom so as to form a pile, which stands at right angles to the warp. The earliest example of knotted-pile carpet was found in a frozen tomb at Pazyryk in Siberia and is now displayed in the Hermitage Museum, St Petersburg in Russia. It was woven in the 4th or 5th century BC. The carpet has a pattern of rosettes similar to those featured on rugs depicted in the reliefs of Assyrian palaces.

The two greatest weaving cultures in history are those of Turkey and Iran. During the 16th century, carpets

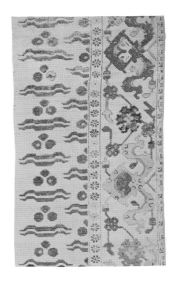

△ Detail of a balls and stripes carpet from Ushak in Turkey, woven in the late 16th century. Some experts think it is based on a leopard skin design, since to ancient Turkoman and Iranian rulers these had talismanic powers.

◁ Detail of the Pazyryk rug, excavated in 1947 in the Altai Mountains of Siberia and datable to the 5th century BC. Like later oriental carpets, it has a central field surrounded by several borders.

◁ The Berlin dragon and phoenix carpet was discovered in an Italian church in 1886. It was probably woven in early 15th-century Anatolia.

▽ Silk animal carpet, woven in Persia during the Safavid period. Both central medallion and all-over carpet designs were woven in the royal workshops.

were sent from these countries to all parts of the known world: from Egypt to North Africa, Spain and Venice, and from there to the rest of Europe. They were also sent eastwards and their popularity spread to India and Turkestan. Islamic courts of the 16th and 17th centuries were notable patrons of the arts. They set up royal workshops, which included textiles and carpets. The rarest and most collectible varieties were woven under the dynasty of the Safavids (1502–1736). Designs include animals, hunting themes, gardens, vases, medallions and so-called Polonaise (Polish) carpets that were woven with

silk and gold threads. Individual variations of this style were developed in neighbouring oriental empires.

The Ottoman court workshops in Turkey and the Mogul court workshops in India also produced many marvellous carpets. The Mogul carpets featured a more naturalistic rendering of plants and animals, whereas the court workshops of the Ottoman empire depicted lusher vegetation and busier looking backgrounds. In Asia Minor during the 16th and 17th centuries, Ushak carpets (with more angular designs and a less extensive range of colours than the Persian carpets) were being exported to

Europe. Holbein depicted many of these carpets in his paintings. European courts also set up royal workshops at this time, producing carpets both in the oriental style as well as developing quite distinctive European designs.

China may have independently developed the craft of carpet-making, but Persian carpets certainly found their way there too. There are many paintings of the time depicting Persian and Turkish carpets and rugs. Egypt and North African countries such as Morocco and Algeria were also influenced. Their carpets are known as Mediterranean carpets. Spain, the first European country to have a distinctive weaving tradition, produced carpets which were often similar to those from North Africa and are also classified as Mediterranean.

By the end of the 17th century, the carpet market in the East had declined, due to political instability in Persia and to the growing taste for European-produced carpets. It did not recover again until the mid-19th century, when their popularity was due not to court patronage but to a wealthier populace who rediscovered their beauty and usefulness. The demand for carpets from the Western market grew steadily by the end of the 19th century and workshops at Peking and Tientsin became associated with Aubusson and other Western-inspired designs. As far back as the 17th century, some designers had created rugs specifically to complement particular architectural or interior style or fashion. In the 19th century, this trend increased quite dramatically, particularly in the West.

▽ A rare Ningxia carpet from the 17th century with geometric medallions all over the field and a border of blue swastika motifs. The swastika is the classic character for 10,000, so the border symbolizes "ten thousand fold happiness".

▷ This Louis Philippe Aubusson, woven c. 1840, is very typical with its dusty yellows and rusty reds and its huge central medallion and myriad daisy flowers.

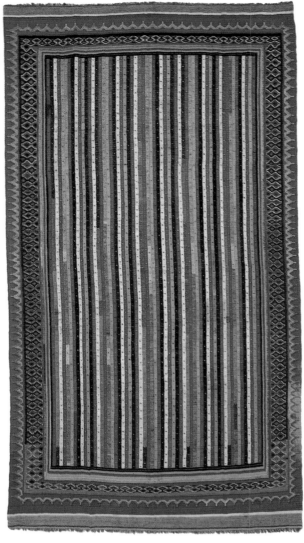

△ This kilim was woven by the Shahsavan tribe in north-west Iran. The design comprises an array of animals in geometric style.

▷▷ This rare Quashq'ai kilim was woven in western Persia, c. 1890. Quashq'ai designs are bold and vibrantly colourful.

FLAT-WEAVE TAPESTRY

Another, more utilitarian type of rug, is woven by tribes all over the world using the flat-weave or tapestry technique. This process produces a strong, versatile textile with the potential for boldly coloured motifs or pictures. These tribal flat-weaves exist in many forms, including kilims, dhurries and the North American Navajo blankets and rugs. These carpets were made primarily for their own use by nomads and permanently settled tribes, but any that were produced in excess of domestic needs were also on sale for many hundreds of years, particularly in the Muslim world. The Turks and the Iranians are the most renowned weavers of these carpets and traditional designs have changed very little over the centuries.

Kilims are the largest group of tribal tapestries in the world. They are quicker to weave and use less wool than knotted-pile carpets, so they are cheaper to produce although, until the middle of this century, Western buyers preferred pile carpets. In India, the equivalent of the kilim is the dhurrie, which is made by the same flat-weaving technique, but usually from cotton rather than wool. Dhurries are duller in colour, more matt in appearance and heavier than kilims. There are many different types, including coarse weaves for bedding and finer weaves to brighten up festive occasions.

TUFTED RUGS

Nowadays, tufted rugs are produced in a few weaving centres. In China these have the same designs, colours and yarns as pile carpets, but they are not hand-knotted and not as long-lasting. They are, however, considerably cheaper as tufting is so much quicker and they are perfectly acceptable for home furnishing, in addition to being much better value than comparable machine-made rugs. In stores the difference between tufted and genuine hand-knotted rugs is not always made clear, so be aware of what you are looking at.

▽ Arts & Crafts carpet specially designed for Draper's Hall in London, woven by Morris & Co. It has a splendid design of bold Indian motifs intertwined with vines.

CONTEMPORARY CARPETS

For the carpet buyer today, there is an enormous choice available – to suit all homes and all pockets. Knotted-pile and flat-woven carpets are still being woven. From Persian thick-pile wool carpets, with their wonderfully glowing reds and blues, to delicate silk carpets from China and the flat- or tapestry-weaves that have been woven by nomadic tribes or cottage workshops all over the world, motifs, dyestuffs and weaving techniques have been passed down from generation to generation ever since weaving first began. Many modern-day weavers still use ancient methods, looms and motifs. The many nomadic and settled tribes – who live in the broad zone of Asia, from the Mediterranean to the Pacific – continue to produce a wide range of the most desirable rugs for the home.

One big difference that has been seen this century is that whereas carpet weaving used to be an indigenous traditional art, designed for local use, it has now become an organized industry supplying the Western market. Vegetable dyes have yielded to chemical dyes (although some workshops are returning to vegetable dyes because that is what some Westerners want). Patterns are designed or adapted to appeal to Western taste. Often, designs are created in the West and weavers in the East are commissioned to produce the finished items. The large demand for export goods means that the yarn and the weaving may not be of the finest quality. However, well-made and designed rugs are still being created and the search for these can be rewarding.

COLLECTIBLE CARPETS

Today the carpet hunter has an enormous choice. Of the two main types of carpet (those with a pile and those which are flat-woven), the most collectible are oriental carpets or fragments. The second-hand and antique market can still offer wonderful old carpets and rugs which have a very special appeal and, if they are in good condition, these can be worth a great deal of money. These may come from anywhere between Turkey and China and most date from the 18th and 19th centuries. Almost all of the early oriental palace carpets are now safely stored in museums. Probably the richest collections are in Berlin, London, New York, Paris and Vienna.

Western carpets, such as Aubusson and Savonnerie, are also collectible. The rugs designed by William Morris, who spearheaded the Arts & Crafts movement and

◁ This is a beautiful example of the wonderful modern designs now being made. It has a lovely castellated border containing colourful abstract shapes.

△ Art Deco, Fauve-inspired Savonnerie carpet attributed to the Parisian Atelier Primavery, woven c. 1926. Its larger-than-life sandwashed flowers provide the perfect foil for its geometric setting. Such 20th-century designs are expensive and greatly sought after by collectors.

produced rugs to counteract the machine-made products that he despised, are eminently collectible today. Some 20th-century rugs are also valuable; those designed by Marian Dorn for modernist houses in the 1930s are very sought after, for instance. However, most modern carpets, such as those made in India, Pakistan, Afghanistan, China and Eastern Europe in traditional designs, although regarded as wonderful assets to the interior decoration of a home, are not seen as quick investment potential. However, unquestionably they lend an advantage to many modern interiors and who knows what their worth will be in another hundred years' time?

One of the main things to look out for is the fineness and quality of the yarn, which is considered to be the essential guide to the quality of a carpet. Because wool is widely available, very durable and takes dyes wonderfully well, carpets with a wool pile are the most generally available of all of the types today and they are fantastically diverse.

Modern factory-made adaptations and reproductions are also widely available and should not be despised: they may not have investment potential but they can provide warmth and colour to the modern home and are remarkably inexpensive.

CARPET DESIGNS AND MOTIFS

Design can be a useful pointer to the origins of a carpet, but centres of trade, migration and intermarriage have spread the range of motifs and designs over a wide area. Motifs are drawn from a number of sources, including religious, cultural and environmental. Many of their meanings are lost in the mists of time, while others have been introduced more recently. Several common themes and motifs appear in rugs that are being produced in places as far apart from the Balkans and Iran to Afghanistan, China and North Africa.

GEOMETRIC AND FLORAL DESIGNS

Oriental carpets are woven in two distinct main styles: geometric and floral. Geometric designs use straight lines to form the various elements whereas floral rugs use curvilinear motifs. The geometric style is primarily the style of tribal and village weaving. Designs are handed down from generation to generation by example and word of mouth. Most geometric styles are concentrated in the Caucasus, Anatolia and Central Asia. Geometric versions of carpets featuring central medallions, i.e. with polygonal medallions, are produced in Anatolia and the Caucasus, whereas carpets with curvilinear-style medallions are more likely to come from Iran.

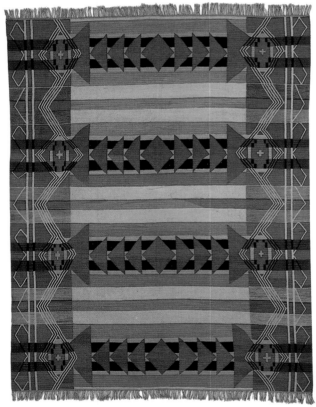

◁ The Chinese dragon motif represents the union of earthly and celestial forces, and the emperor.

△ A splendid Anatolian flat-weave featuring a geometric design in glowing red, sand and green.

△ Persian curvilinear floral carpet with an intricate all-over design of tiny flowers.

▽ This is a typical Belouch prayer rug with a squared-arch mihrab and a stylized tree-of-life.

Curvilinear designs were probably introduced towards the end of the 15th century and were then developed in Persia during the 16th century. They originate from the Persian view of the garden as paradise, which is one of the most deeply rooted images in the culture of their hot and arid land. Persian garden style has influenced gardens throughout the centuries and their carpets often mirror this. Asymmetrical knots are often used (although not always) because they are irregular and well suited to reproducing curved lines. Designs for such carpets are created by a master designer and the weavers follow a pattern or cartoon.

Both geometric and floral carpets are usually designed to established rules of composition: their patterns involve every part of the surface area, which is divided into a central area or field with corners and borders.

PRAYER RUGS

The prayer rug has been used in Muslim countries for centuries and it provides a clean spot for worship. Each rug has an arch-shaped niche, known as a mihrab. Many of the rugs that are woven in Anatolia are still based on this form, which is also the basis for most Belouch and some other tribal rugs. The saph is a multiple prayer rug with several mihrabs placed side by side.

Predating Islam and Christianity, the tree-of-life symbol is often used together with garden and prayer rug designs. There are several workshops in Anatolia, India and Pakistan as well as Iran that are producing sophisticated and ornate versions of this design and more stylized versions are used in tribal rugs.

PICTORIAL CARPETS

Pictorial (people and animal motif) rugs are less common in the East than in the West. They are based on everyday life, history or mythology. Persian Shahs, like royalty the world over, enjoyed seeing themselves depicted as brave and noble hunters on horseback. These rugs are still produced in Iranian workshops, but most of them now come from India and Pakistan.

CHINESE DESIGNS

Chinese carpets differ from those of any other Eastern rug-producing country, largely because the influence of Islam has had little impact on the designs, although today China produces carpets based on traditional Persian designs that have no connection with China. Symbols are important in Chinese culture. Contemporary Chinese rug designers have taken elements from Taoism and Buddhism, as well as from paintings, ceramics and embroidery. Rugs from the Turkoman region (between China and the Islamic weaving regions) use designs that have been influenced by both cultures and it is not always easy to identify from which area these originated. Some designs are used in several different regions and similar patterns, with tonal and thematic changes, often appear.

INDIVIDUAL MOTIFS

It is impossible to say where and when most motifs evolved. Some are clearly based on religious symbolism; others may simply be stylized depictions of plant forms. Some motifs are recognizable as the plants, animals, etc. after which they are modelled. Others have become so stylized that it is impossible to find any connection at all. Serious research into the origins of the meaning of carpet patterns and motifs has only just begun. However, it is useful to be able to name the various motifs and some of the most common ones are given here. There are usually many different geometric and curvilinear forms of each motif.

GUL

Persian for flower, a gul is a lozenge-shaped motif arranged in vertical rows. It is actually a stylized flower head but looks rather like a squashed medallion. Gul motifs spread throughout much of Central Asia and they are the basis of many Turkoman carpet designs, often being repeated in an all-over pattern. They are closely associated with Bokhara, a traditional marketing centre for rugs. The gul is seen in nomadic rugs (which have their own tribal guls) and also in workshop-produced carpets woven in Afghanistan, Anatolia, the Caucasus and Pakistan. There are numerous different types of gul.

MEDALLION

A dominant motif which forms the main design element of a carpet. Used mainly in the Caucasus, Anatolia and Persia, these come in many forms. They are either used individually in the centre of the rug or several may be used across the rug. The latter have an heraldic quality and are known as amulets.

BOTEH

A paisley pattern formed by a fat, almond-shaped motif tapering to a curl at the top. Most frequently seen in the mir-i-boteh configuration, after the Persian village which was renowned for rugs in this design.

Guls

Amulet/medallion

Boteh

Herati

Turkoman gul motif

Caucasian hooked medallion

Persian boteh motif

HERATI

Single floral-headed design with a diamond framework and four curling leaves. It is sometimes known as fish-in-the-pond or mahi (Persian for fish). It is often used to make meander border patterns. (A meander is an undulating motif in linear form, often used in border designs.) The herati motif is made by many workshops, village and nomadic groups throughout Iran. It is rarely found outside Iran, though India now produces rugs in traditional herati patterns. Mina-khani is similar to herati, but consists of a single flower within a diamond lattice, which has four flower heads at each of its points.

TREE-OF-LIFE

This is an ancient religious symbol predating both Islam and Christianity. It represents the connection between this world and paradise.

STAR

Star motifs include the eight-pointed star, the cruciform star and cross (the star/diamond). They are found on kilims from all regions.

SWASTIKA

An ancient design that can be found in America, Europe, India and China. The Chinese fret is based on interlocking swastikas and is often used in borders.

SHOU AND FU

Shou and fu symbolize long life and good luck. Most symbolic Chinese characters are referred to as shou or fu, regardless of their form.

ANIMALS, BIRDS AND PLANTS

A huge variety of pictorial motifs can be found throughout the weaving regions, both stylized and highly naturalistic.

CLOUDBAND

Clouds are used in Anatolian, Persian, Turkoman and Chinese carpets. They may be used individually or interlinked to form a meandering border.

Tree-of-life   Stars   Swastikas   Shou   Fu

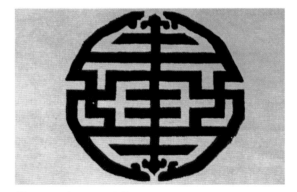

Chinese shou medallion

Chinese pictorial motif

Caucasian medallion containing cloudband motifs

INTERIOR INSPIRATIONS

Beautiful carpets and rugs are perhaps the most aesthetically pleasing, warming and humanizing elements that can be added to an interior. Though bold in colour and positive in design, most rugs will fit into almost any interior, miraculously adding to its elegance and charm without competing for attention, but amiably blending in – although where a focus is required, a well-placed and well-chosen rug can command attention. Even the most distinctive carpets will adapt to different styles of home, rooms and decorative purposes, such as wall hangings, throws, cushions and even upholstery.

For centuries, nomadic peoples have used their weavings to supply them with luxurious furnishings for their far from primitive lifestyles. Flat-weaves have been used as camel and pony trappings, carrying bags for bedding, clothes and food, floor coverings, divisions within the tent, seating – and much more. In Western homes, too, they can be used in a great number of different ways.

▷▷ The simple, strong design of the deep apricot rug coordinates with the paler apricot of the sofa and the strong, simple shapes of a modern living room.

▷ The rich, browny red rug complements the natural stone floor, wooden dresser and round table in a traditional dining room.

Rugs are available in many different sizes, designs, colours, textures and weaving techniques: some are so sturdy and stiff that they just ask to be put on the floor, while others are so delicate that they can be hung as pictures on the wall. The colours of both hand-knotted and flat-woven carpets and rugs (although rich and vivid) are, in general, so subtle that they can be used in almost any interior. They will complement a home that already glows with colour, while lifting a somewhat bland interior to something quite out of the ordinary.

DISPLAYING AND USING CARPETS AND RUGS

Be expansive about the way in which you use rugs and carpets; they don't have to be confined to the floor. Any insight into traditional uses may inspire creative placing in your own home. The Chinese, for example, designed carpets specifically to fit around pillars; there was no vertical border pattern and a design, such as a dragon, formed a continuous image when wrapped around a column. In the yurts (or tents) of the nomadic tribes of Asia, rich, warmly coloured weavings provided insulation against the harsh winds of the Asian steppes.

You can also diversify from traditional uses: Ensis rugs (that serve as tent entrance curtains) are less stiff than many others and can be adapted for use as throws. Prayer rugs are essentially small (for easy transportation) so that the devout Muslim can carry one around with him as a handy, unsullied surface on which to pray. They are ideal for filling in narrow spaces between large rugs and for use as hangings or bedside rugs. Or take a tip from the Iranian Kurdish and Balouchi tribes whose square korsi rugs covered charcoal braziers or bread ovens when not in use and served as a

◁ This room, with its natural terracotta tile flooring and white-washed walls, has been brought to life by the use of several flat-weaves, on the floor, table and wall.

▷ Kilims make excellent table rugs, being good-looking, flexible and protective. This one is used in a study, where it looks particularly good with the leather-bound books.

△ A small flat-woven rug provides texture and colour coordination in a modern, disciplined living room.

◁ An Aubusson carpet under the refectory table and a pale-coloured runner in the hall complement the embroidered upholstery in this panelled interior.

warm, heavy family blanket in the harsh mountain winters. In Scandinavia, pile-weaving served as cloaks and sleigh robes by day and blankets or bed coverings by night, and the serapes or blankets of Mexicans and the Navajo Indians from south-west America were similarly dual purpose. Brightly coloured and striped modern versions of these serapes can serve as light-wear rugs or throws.

FLOOR CARPETS

Carpets designed for use on the floor should be up to the job. In general, the harder the wear, the denser the weave

should be; and if you are using a flat-woven kilim, try not to choose one made with the slit-weave technique if it is going to have heavy boots treading all over it because it is bound to be less robust. Any rug that is used on the floor should be thick and tough enough not to ruck or turn up at the corners, otherwise people will easily trip over it. Carpets for use in wet areas, such as a bath or shower room, should always be small in size so that they can be easily dried. If the bathroom is used by children (or anyone else who is liable to splash or spill a lot of water), then don't use an oriental carpet here.

WALL CARPETS

Rugs make very splendid wall hangings. Hand-knotted rugs will be more difficult to hang because of their weight, but any rug can be hung from a rod fixed to the wall.

USING CARPETS AS CUSHIONS AND UPHOLSTERY

Carpets that are too worn to use in their entirety can still be useful if they are cut up and the good pieces used to make cushion covers. When several of these are heaped up together on a sofa or divan or used individually on dining chairs, they add immediate interest to a room. Kilims make one of the most durable and good-looking upholstery fabrics and they look particular good on simple chairs and sofas and on ottoman stools, both large and small.

▷▷ Quashq'ai kilims and rugs have been used with great effect – on the floor, on the bed itself and on the chair – in a converted barn with splendid beams. Even the curtains are made from a printed kilim-effect fabric.

▷ A boldly patterned kilim is complemented by a pile cushion cover, giving a sumptuous feeling to an otherwise pale bedroom.

Carpets that are already a little worn – or include silk in their make up or are otherwise delicate for some reason – should either be fitted in very light traffic areas (such as a bedroom or little used part of a living room) or be used as table covers or hung on the wall. All carpets and rugs should have an underlay to protect them from any damage caused by being squeezed between both floor and shoes.

ENTRANCE HALLS

A handmade rug will immediately transform any entrance hall into a welcoming area. Here, the most important thing to bear in mind is that the rug should be able to withstand considerable wear. Dust and dirt are among the most damaging things for a rug, so make sure there is a substantial doormat positioned where people can wipe their feet before they reach the rug. Carpet matting is available by the metre or yard, so there is no reason to skimp on it. Any rug that is chosen for the hall must be both durable and easily cleaned. A densely woven rug would be ideal, preferably in darkish colours that will not show up any dirt. And it is very important to use underlay on tiles or wood floors to prevent the carpet from slipping or rucking up and also to protect it from being squeezed too hard between both shoes and floor.

Long runners are ideal for a long, narrow corridor where they can complement the shape of the space. There is no need, however, to stick to just the one rug in the hall. If you don't have a long enough rug, then put two or three together to provide the same welcoming warmth and colour. A narrow space looks better if it is mirrored on one side and you could even hang a rug opposite the mirror to give a stronger feeling of warmth. Slit-weave kilims, although not the best sort of rug to have on the floor, look marvellous when they are hung on the wall, adding to the richness and warmth of the space, particularly if they are reflected in a mirror.

A wider entrance hall will look better with a shorter, rectangular rug (or several small ones). And if they are placed under a hall table, where they are less likely to get dirty, these can even be paler in colour.

△ An Afghan kilim has been used to provide an unusual cover for this upholstered ottoman, which stands on a pile rug – not matching, but with much the same feeling.

▷▷ The look of the upright piano in this hallway is given a stylish softening element by a long runner bearing small, camel motifs.

▷ A kilim and Turkman tent band have been cut up and used to create an effective and unusual stair carpet in a traditional townhouse.

▷▷ A floral carpet provides the perfect foil for a pretty, traditionally furnished room with pale upholstery and draped curtains.

▽ This small conversation corner would be uncompromizingly formal and minimalist, were it not for the cane chairs and the texture and deep colours of the flat-woven rugs.

LIVING ROOMS

Rugs can be used to give a different emphasis of colour to a living room. One large, single Persian carpet can be the focal point of a formal room whereas a smaller one can be used to break up an expanse of floor or carpet. Several smaller rugs can be used to fill gaps in the spacing of furniture and many rugs, all juxtaposed and overlapping, can produce a varied, yet unifying effect in a room. A rich, deep red rug looks lovely when laid in front of a fireplace where the wool pile will catch the light in a particularly attractive and subtle way.

But, of course, a rug need not be placed on the floor at all. When hung on the wall, a rug can be quite as attractive

as a painting. Flat–woven rugs can be used on small tables and even pile carpets can be placed on larger tables, provided the pile is not too long and the carpet is not too heavy to hang over the edges. Flat–weaves make excellent upholstery fabrics and look very good on large, simple designs of armchair and sofa, and on ottoman stools too. Undamaged fragments of old and worn rugs make good cushion covers. They nearly always look best when several cushions are thrown on a sofa together, where their patterns and colours can really lift the look of a room. Rugs may be used as throws if they are pliable and soft enough. Moroccan tribal weaves, for example, are suitable for this treatment, since they are often quite loosely woven.

◁ Kilim-style fabrics work well with upholstery. This one has been used on an overstuffed sofa. Although not matching, the bold fabric goes well with the pile rug on the floor.

△ This intricately patterned carpet, with its wide borders and dark centre field, is the perfect companion for an ornate mirror and traditional gateleg table.

▷ This beautiful abstract carpet from the mid-1920s is an excellent choice to complement a spare, modernist interior. The rich rusts, olive greens and dusty pinks show up well against the natural pine flooring under a wash of sunlight.

▷ Rugs, such as this dark blue, red and white Persian pile rug, can turn a conventional bathroom into a much more personal room, particularly when used with a traditional bathroom suite and wood panelling round the bath.

▽ A small, simple yet elegant kilim, in pale yellow and orange, lifts the somewhat heavy effect produced by the dark, wooden refectory table and Tudor-style dining chairs in this traditional dining room.

BATHROOMS

Many carpets are suitable for bathroom use and they can certainly turn one of the more utilitarian areas of the home into a place of sensuous pleasure. However, if the bathroom suffers from condensation or gets saturated by splashes of water seeping from badly sealed shower cabinets, then don't expect a rug to last for any length of time. One great enemy of rugs is water, which leads to rot and to brittleness of the yarns, and both of these things are difficult – if not impossible – to put right.

KITCHENS

Placed in front of the sink and work surfaces in the kitchen, a warm rug can be very welcome and it can certainly help to lessen the somewhat clinical aspect of many kitchen layouts. You will need a rug that is hard-wearing, easy to clean and in dark colours. Long, narrow runners are not now commonly used in Western homes, but they can complement a length of cupboards and appliances in a kitchen. In a square or U-shaped kitchen, choose a shape that fits the space. The rug for such a situation must be heavy and robust. Most kitchens have ceramic, vinyl or other easily cleaned flooring, which is often very slippery, so it is of extra importance to have a good underlay fitted to stop the rug from sliding around. It must lie flat, with no wrinkles to trip up the cook. Wool, contrary to what many people suppose, is easy to clean and cooking spills, if dealt with immediately, are easier to remove from wool than from cotton. Wall hangings are not so appropriate for kitchen use since they will absorb the grease and food particles rising in the cooking steam.

Dining Rooms

Carpets with a central medallion design work particularly well in a dining room, but you must choose your carpet carefully. If you have babies or small children, the rug will need constant cleaning and will inevitably suffer. Crumbs, like dust, are not good for textiles. Any rug that you use should be so tightly woven and durable that it will withstand frequent vacuuming and spot removing. It should be large enough to fit under the table without the legs of chairs catching the edges of the rug. Make sure you use a

▷ Red is a popular colour for a formal dining room and it is beautifully provided here by a large, Turkish pile carpet with ornate corners and border and a small, overall pattern.

▷ A hand-knotted carpet adds the final touch of splendour to this elegant room, where everything is carefully chosen and designed to reinforce the room's proportions and arched windows.

△ Textiles are an important element in this bedroom design and small Persian kilims have been used generously to add to the textural feel and colour.

good underlay: table and chair legs can cause the carpet to wear unevenly. A narrow rug can look good in front of a sideboard, if the room is large enough. Again, make sure it is sturdy and won't wrinkle. A good underlay can help to prevent this from happening. The dining room is often a good place in which to hang a knotted rug or kilim, rather than a painting or print. It is a place where subtle lighting can give an attractive glow to the colours of a rug as well as enhance the textures of the weaving.

CHILDREN'S ROOMS

Kilims are ideal for children's rooms insofar as they are warm, friendly, colourful and inexpensive. But any carpet makes it difficult to set up train sets, build bricks or other constructions for which a smooth floor makes a better base. So for young children, a small prayer rug by the bed may be a better bet. Older children and teenagers who have any sense of the aesthetics of their room will welcome kilims as floor and bed coverings, floor cushions or wall

◁ The richness of the red drapes surrounding this large, four-poster bed is echoed in the intricate patterning and deep colouring of the Persian carpet on the floor.

▽ The country charm of this room is provided by the pale wood, floral walls and green and white runner that ties the various elements together.

hangings, depending on personal taste and space. Tribal bags, often woven to carry salt and other household items, can be used as specialist storage for socks or papers – or in a simple decorative capacity, placed over the arms of chairs or hung on the wall.

Bedrooms

A strongly coloured, intricately patterned wool or cotton rug is a perfect foil for a farmhouse bedroom with a brass bedstead or a masculine bedroom with Victorian mahogany wardrobes and polished leather shoes, and it can also complement and strengthen a bedroom scheme based on dimity floral patterns and frilled curtain headings. Pile rugs or flat-weave kilims will complement patchwork quilts, modern fitted cupboards, antique furniture and, indeed, practically any scheme. For guest bedrooms, they are ideal for providing a warm atmosphere immediately upon arrival. Strange rooms often feel a little cold and, placed on the floor, wall or bed, a rug is immediately friendly and welcoming.

△ Natural flooring makes a good background for the attractive rug at the end of the bed in this simple and comfortable bedroom.

STYLE
DIRECTORY

ELEMENTS OF CARPET STYLE

Pattern, colour, weave, texture, shape and size all contribute to the overall style of a carpet and its effect on a decorative scheme. The majority of oriental carpets are rectangular and are composed according to a long-established set of rules. Their layouts generally consist of a central field framed by one or, more frequently, several borders. The field may be open (undecorated), but generally contains one or more medallions or an all-over decoration. It is useful to have a basic understanding of these elements and how they are combined when assessing the wide variety of carpet styles available.

COLOURS AND DESIGNS

Carpets usually have a dominant colour, which is an important factor to consider in selecting a carpet. Since there is such a richness of choice in the colours of carpets, you will almost certainly be able to find a rug that fits in with a particular colour scheme if you wish, but a carpet that picks up the overall colour scheme of a room only in the detail of its design could also be very effective. The mood of a design as a whole may be even more important than the colour. Whether you wish to have elegant formal arabesques and curvilinear designs such as those that can be found in many Persian and Indian carpets or the more geometric Caucasian designs, will depend on the formality and general mood of the room itself. In general, well-proportioned rooms with tall ceilings will give expensive, court-type carpets the environment in which they look best. Designs with a definite central medallion or those that are largely figurative deserve to be placed in a central position where their picture can be appreciated. Overall designs and carpets with one main overall colour, embellished with small motifs here and there, will be more suited to a more eclectic and less formal interior.

TEXTURES, PILES AND WEAVES

Texture, too, must be taken into account. A deep, soft, wool pile catches the light in a very different way to a cotton pile or a flat-weave. Even turning a hand-knotted carpet round so that the pile is facing in a different direction will affect the way that it looks. Different wools react to light in various ways and some of those with a high sheen can easily be mistaken for silk at first glance. A woollen kilim gives a very different feeling to a cotton dhurrie. Personal taste has much to do with choice, but it is very useful to get accustomed to looking at rugs with these qualities in mind, when considering something for your own home. The practical aspects of wear are, of course, just as important. When judging a rug, look at the fineness of the knotting, the quality of the materials and the intricacy and symmetrical balance of the design.

Major border

Minor border

Central medallion

Decorated field

Corner (spandrel)

Fringe

Full-field decoration
(geometric)

Minor border

Major border

Fringe

Full-field decoration
(repeating motifs)

Minor border

Major border

Major border

Minor border

Central medallion

Open field

Corner (spandrel)

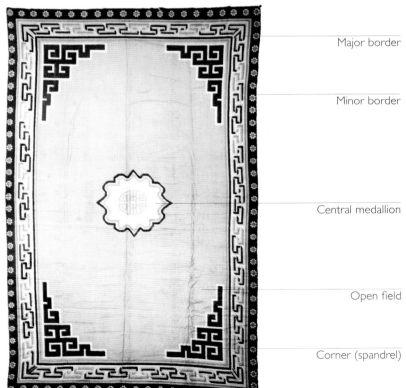

IRAN

Although the first carpets to be purchased by Europeans were from Turkey and became known as "Turkey carpets", today most people think of oriental carpets as "Persian carpets" and it is the magnificent Persian court carpets of the 16th and 17th centuries that have had most influence on later designs in all weaving regions.

Persian carpets from the Safavid dynasty (1502–1736) are the most magnificent and highly sought after. The Safavids set up royal workshops for the production of carpets and other textiles, and the carpets produced at this time include beautiful animal and hunting designs. Isfahan was one of the capitals of Persia before Tehran was created in the 18th century and the finest rugs traditionally come from Isfahan. Many of the early court carpets can still be seen in museums and occasionally carpets – or fragments of them – may come up for auction. They were often woven with warp threads of cotton with a cotton and/or silk weft. Persian designs

Today, Iran (Persia) is the home of the most numerous and varied carpet-weaving groups in the world, who produce hand-knotted carpets and kilims on tribal looms, both in villages and urban workshops.

have been woven in carpet-producing countries in the East including India, Pakistan, the Balkans and even China, which has a very different cultural background to Persia.

Persian carpets are woven in wool, cotton and silk, and gold and silver threads were occasionally used in court carpets. Designs are highly complex and calligraphic, with the emphasis on design and curvilinear lines that are used to interpret the essentially poetical leanings of the region and the love of flowers and gardens. The particular form of Islam which dominates in Iran allows for greater freedom of expression than that of Anatolia and the human figure is an important element in many Persian carpets. A great number of colours are used in each carpet, but in a delicate and balanced juxtaposition. Nomadic carpets are, of course, less complex and more stylized than the court carpets; they are mostly in geometric, rather than curvilinear, patterns.

THE SOUTHERN TRIBES

SOUTHERN IRAN HAS several weaving regions and although they all have distinguishing features, similar designs, motifs and colours are often to be found in each region. The Fars region is vast and two nomadic populations are responsible for the rug weaving in the area: the Quashq'ai and the Kamseh. In these two groups the weaving is very similar and rugs are often referred to as Fars or Shiraz (the city where they are marketed).

The southern tribal confederation consists of five main tribes: Quashq'ai, Bakhtiari, Afshar, Luri and Kamseh (which is Persian for "five"). Caucasian influences can be seen in all of their designs, which include the boteh, medallion, flora and pole-medallion motifs. They are usually woven with the Senneh (asymmetrical) knot and are often based on a central medallion, with small geometrical motifs filling the field. Fairly narrow borders are often used. Generally speaking, Quashq'ai are more likely to be curvilinear and tend to use brighter colours, whereas the Kamseh are more inclined to be geometric and to use darker colours.

CHARACTERISTICS

Woven by nomads and semi-nomads; extremely attractive; Bakhtiaris are among the most collectible examples of contemporary Persian tribal weaving and Afshars are the most diverse. Older Quashq'ai rugs are considered the best of the nomadic weaving and today's rugs are among the most attractive and technically superb. Gabbehs were originally woven in undyed wools, but today's products for the Western market have large expanses of plain, bright colours with the occasional small motif.

WEAR

Normally woven with cotton warp and weft and a short to medium wool pile, all these rugs are robust, good-looking and they make excellent buys. The better, more finely knotted examples will surely become collectible in the future. Some (e.g. Bakhtiaris) have somewhat loosely packed wefts with a medium pile with a weave that varies from coarse to medium. Gabbehs are coarsely woven and are usually the cheapest versions.

HOME USE

These attractive, hard-wearing rugs have many uses in the home, either grouped together to give a particular feeling to a room or as a focus of attention. They should stand up well to quite hard wear, provided they are given a good underlay and are kept free of dirt.

△ A 19th-century Fars rug, woven by the Kashkuli tribe, who are one of the Quashq'ai confederation and known for their particularly fine work.

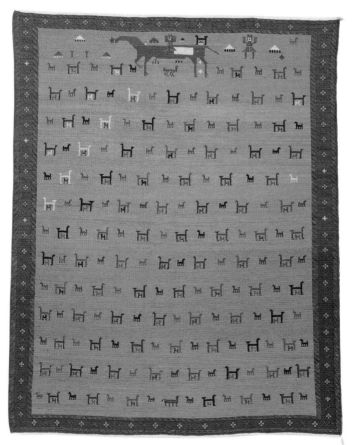

△ This modern rug has a typically rich, yellowy field and a darker, narrow border. The design is of a rich Iranian man (at the top of the rug) with his herd of horses.

▽ A spider carpet, so-called because of its spider-like design, has characteristic small animal figures around the border. It has been woven by the nomadic Quashq'ai confederation of tribes. The attractive variation in background colour is known as abrash.

Some Afshar rugs follow tribal tradition while others follow the ornamental motifs of the city workshops nearby. Borders are decorated with stylized rosettes and vines. Backgrounds tend to be dark with a contrasting paler blue, white, red, yellow and green. Bakhtiari carpets are often woven in rows of squares, octagons and diamonds, each containing stylized plants. The most popular example is the panelled garden design. Luri carpets are extremely varied with stylized plant motifs in grids and tiny geometric motifs in rows. Reds and blues predominate. Finally, gabbehs are among the most primitive of all Persian tribal rugs. They use good quality wool and the best items have a definite charm.

△ A Bakhtiari carpet with a design of European flowers, following in the tradition of the city workshops. A strong European influence can also be seen in the large medallions.

◁ An Afshar rug, decorated in the tribal tradition, with stylized rosettes and vases. The border is typical in its dark background with contrasting red, pale blue and yellow colours.

IRAN

HERIZ

CHARACTERISTICS

Heriz carpets are famous for their boldly heraldic schemes in shades of brick red, burnt orange, deep blues, ivory, yellow ochre and their secondary colours of pale reds and blues. They are among the most easily recognized of all the Persian designs. Heriz are woven in a number of large sizes but not often in the form of small rugs.

WEAR

Heriz carpets are durable and reasonably priced. The number of knots to the square inch is not particularly high but Heriz are compact and hard-wearing, and are made of very good quality wool which is usually clipped to a low or medium pile. They are generally recognized as among the best of the more coarsely woven Persian carpets.

HOME USE

These bright red rugs, with their bold motifs, deserve to be given a place of honour in the home and could brighten up a dining room or a living room, although they require an interior scheme of some confidence and panache.

HERIZ IS THE best known of a number of villages in a district of north-west Iran that stretches to Tabriz and its carpets are superior in quality to others created in the region. The silk carpets that were woven there in the second half of the 19th and early 20th centuries were unsurpassed. Very large woollen carpets were woven at that time too, but these rarely come up at auction.

Modern Heriz carpets are of coarser yarn so the number of knots is fairly low. Nevertheless, they wear extremely well. Although the city of Tabriz is so near, Heriz rugs are quite different in character and retain an identity very much their own. The dominant composition is based on an enormous and powerful angular central medallion in a field of geometric floral motifs with the corners echoing the medallion. Surrounding villages produce variations on this theme and many produce well-made, tightly woven rugs in curvilinear medallions and corner designs.

▷ This long, narrow runner was woven in Bakhshaiesh, a small village near Heriz. It has an overall boteh design, with more widely spaced boteh motifs in the border.

▽ This carpet translates classical Persian floral motifs into geometric forms and spreads the colour over wide areas.

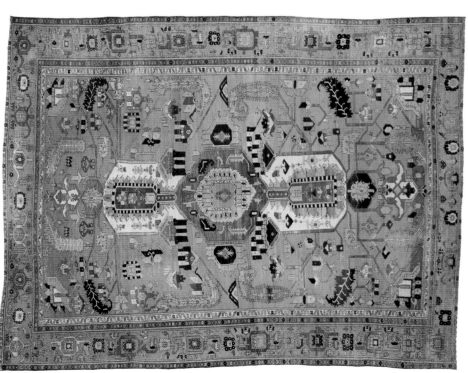

▷ This carpet was woven *c.* 1830 in the small village of Bakhshaiesh, whose carpets are renowned for their soft colours and bold patterns.

△ This splendid Heriz carpet, woven *c.* 1890, has a golden, very intricate field with a startlingly deep blue niche, in a design traditionally woven in Ghiordes.

▷ This Heriz rug, woven in the 1880s, features a delightful crocodile design. Weavers in the Heriz area were able to produce complex designs from simple drawings, without the use of detailed cartoons.

CITY WORKSHOPS

CITIES, SUCH AS Tabriz, Isfahan, Kerman, Kashan and Meshed, are historically the largest in Iran and the most important centres of trade. During the "court" period (late 16th to early 18th centuries), finely knotted silk carpets, with gold and silver threads woven in, were woven for the Safavid nobility. A court miniaturist created the designs that were then converted to cartoons and used as models for the weavers. Persian artists, constantly searching for something new, devised more and more complex designs and often introduced religious and poetic verses into a rug.

Court carpet workshops closed in the early 18th century, when the towns were occupied by the Afghans. In the 1920s, however, workshop carpets from these cities began to appear in Europe again and they are still among the most outstanding oriental carpets that it is possible to find. The pile is cut down very low so that the contours of the pattern emerge quite clearly.

CHARACTERISTICS

These carpets are made specifically for sale, both at local markets and for export abroad, and employ many labourers. Workshop weavers weave to order; it is the masters who create the cartoons (pattern charts) or models. They use a curvilinear style with elaborate designs and perfectly balanced colours. City workshop carpets are expertly woven, with no variation in tension or individual aberrations in the design.

WEAR

These carpets, in spite of the delicacy of their patterns, the fineness of the yarns and the low cut of the pile, are very hard-wearing and, with reasonable treatment, can be expected to last for many years.

HOME USE

Although city carpets are robust, it would be madness to use them in parts of the house that get a heavy and dirty flow of traffic. They really need to be placed in an environment that will complement their elegance, sophistication and beauty. A living room or dining room, or a large and spacious boudoir or bedroom, would certainly do them justice. Colours too will fade if they are placed where they will be in direct sunlight for a significant part of the day.

△ This wonderful silk carpet, with its meticulously woven animals and plants, is one of the finest examples in existence today of a 16th-century (Safavid period) city carpet.

△ This unusual carpet was woven in Isfahan during the 1900s. A strong European influence can clearly be seen in the overall design of the flowers.

▽ A fine city carpet, *c.* 1890, showing the characteristically separate motifs and the rich, red field often used in these carpets.

Almost all city workshop carpets have a bright ground and symmetrical design. Medallions are often lobed, with eight or 16 points.

Best-quality carpets are not normally woven in very large sizes because these take several years to make. Many city carpets are renowned for their fine detailing. The pictorial rugs are justly famous and include the four seasons (an allegory of the life of an Azerbaijanian peasant), ruins of mosques and palaces (of which there are many in the area), and magnificent vases and bowls found by archaeologists. Meshed carpets usually date from the late 19th and early 20th centuries and the most common design is the medallion, usually round or elongated in shape and decorated with pendants and floral motifs. They are sometimes made with the jufti knot, which originated in the region. The coarser qualities are not particularly hard-wearing.

▷ This carpet, woven by the Ziegler company specifically for the European market in the late 19th century, has a red outer surround to match the main field and a design of mainly geometric flowers.

▷ This delightful carpet was woven *c.* 1900 in Tabriz. Produced in a modern city workshop, the design is based on a 17th-century vase design from Kerman.

▽ This carpet was woven in the 1890s and features an all-over pattern of European-style flowers, although the dark colouring is more Persian in mood.

△ A fine Laver Kerman rug, woven *c.* 1890. The term Laver is used to denote the highest quality Kerman carpets, which can originate anywhere in the Kerman region, not just in the village of Ravar from which the term Laver is derived.

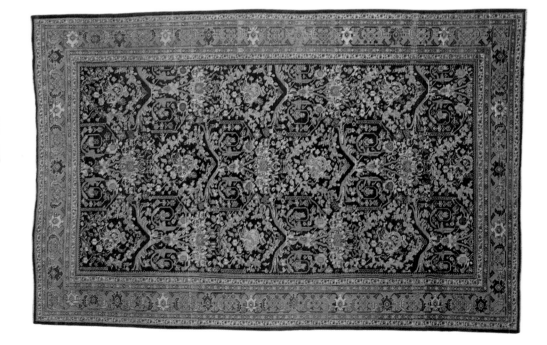

◁ This rare Tabriz carpet, woven *c.* 1890, shows the unusual designs and pale colouring owed to the influence of French Aubussons.

▽ A very fine Tabriz carpet, woven *c.* 1890, showing strong European influence in its pale and subtle colouring. The medallion design is framed typically with several borders in a variety of widths, each containing small floral motifs.

△ This lovely tile-pattern garden carpet was woven in Tabriz *c.* 1890. The design simulates a Persian garden, separated into four orderly sections, with each section subdivided into "tiles" containing floral elements.

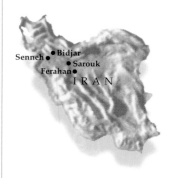

CHARACTERISTICS

Kurdistan sheep have long, tough wool to keep them warm in the mountains. The pile is inclined to lack the rich animal fat of the sheep on the plains. It is shaved as short as possible, and sticks straight up and does not reflect the light as some other pile carpets do. This lack of lustre is compensated for by the pattern, which emerges with great clarity.

WEAR

These thick, heavy carpets, of a nomadic or tribal nature, originate mostly from mountain villages and are usually of excellent standards of workmanship, with a very good quality wool pile clipped short or medium long. They use a cotton warp and weft. These are rugs from mountain villages south of Tehran and bordering onto Turkey and they have always been woven in various places in Kurdistan.

HOME USE

There is a wide variation in the weaving from the different villages in this area and their uses in the home are innumerable. Coarser weaves can be used for quite hard wear in the hall, the kitchen or the bathroom and would also look good in a work-room or a child's room. The finer rugs can be hung on a wall, but they can be used on the floor too, with a piece of suitable underlay fitted beneath them.

VILLAGE WEAVES

THE KURDISH TOWN of Senneh (now Sanandaj) lies in the mountains some miles from the frontier with Iraq. Here some of the thinnest and most sophisticated rugs you can find are woven – quite different to the thick, heavy carpets that are woven in many places in Kurdistan. The pile yarn, warp and weft threads are all extremely thin and the knot count is very high. The Persian asymmetrical knot is known as the Senneh knot. Senneh is a small town with comparatively few weavers and manufacture takes a long time because the rugs are so fine that production is limited. There are few variations in patterns, which mainly consist of pink roses, herati and mir-i-boteh motifs. Roses and boteh are woven in rows over the whole rug, while the herati motifs are used in medallions and the four corners. The predominant colour in early rugs is indigo with plenty of subdued red; late 19th- and early 20th-century rugs are usually cream, soft red and pale green.

Sarouk rugs are good quality, with the pile wool clipped short or medium-long. The designs are separated into traditional and American patterns. Traditional designs include the boteh and herati motifs, but the most impressive is the medallion and corner scheme. Early 20th-century American designs feature large floral sprays which radiate outward from a central medallion. Ferahan carpets were the finest in west-central Iran in the 19th century and the name was synonymous with the herati pattern (a rhomboid surrounded by four small fishes).

◁ An excellent quality Sarouk carpet, c. 1890, with typical design. A European influence can be seen in the floral details.

◁ An exceptional Bidjar carpet, *c.* 1890. Bidjar is a small village that is renowned for the heaviness and durability of its rugs and the deep reds and blues of its designs.

△ An expensive and rare Ferahan carpet, characterized by a field filled with rows of floral motifs, with boteh motifs used in the border.

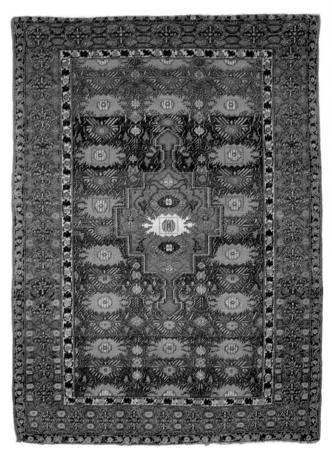

◁ A Bidjar carpet, *c.* 1880, in an overall design of European flowers and with the colours somewhat toned down by the addition of green.

▷ The town of Senneh has become famous throughout the world for its fine rugs and carpets, woven in cottage workshops. This one is in typical indigos and reds.

TURKEY

Turkey is the name now given to the carpet-making region that was once known as Anatolia. Carpets from Turkey were probably brought into Europe via Venice in the 16th and 17th centuries. There are portraits of several famous 16th-century personalities, including King Henry VIII, standing on carpets that are painted in such detail as to be recognizably of Turkish origin. Enough Turkish carpets have survived from the 15th century onwards to give a good idea of their history, and the layers of rugs, donated by local weavers to Turkish mosques, constitute a wonderful archive of weaving over the centuries.

Turkish rugs of recent times fall into two main groups. These are the large hard-wearing, coarsely knotted carpets made in factories, primarily for export to the West, and the smaller rugs and kilims, many being prayer rugs, that were made on domestic looms. Turkey is the largest and most consistent supplier of kilims to

Carpets from Turkey were probably the first to be introduced to Europe, as early as the 16th century. The result was that all hand-knotted carpets were called "Turkey carpets", no matter where they were woven.

the West. Workshop carpets derive their designs from Turkish, Caucasian, Persian and other diverse sources, and many of them are known by the collective name of Smyrna carpets, while others take their names from the places of manufacture, such as Adkhisar, Demirci, Ghiordes, Hereke, Kayseri, Sivas, Sparta and Ushak.

Since the late 1970s, the Turkish authorities and kilim producers have joined forces to restructure their weaving industry, so that it now combines traditional weaving standards and motifs with modern production and marketing techniques. In some cases, the weavers have been encouraged to return to using traditional dyes and materials and to form their own local marketing cooperatives. The result has been a real improvement in the quality of the rugs being woven in the region, and the weavers are able to produce reasonably priced carpets while earning more than when they were working for a contractor.

• Hereke   • Sivas
• Ushak   • Kayseri
T U R K E Y

CHARACTERISTICS

Very fine silk and wool rugs, woven in intricate designs with repeating and intertwining floral elements and rich, deep colours; classic Ottoman prayer rug designs. Silk rugs are woven in shades of red, blue and ivory. Rugs of 7 x 10ft (2 x 1.5m) may be produced, with accents in gilded thread or artificial gold.

WEAR

In both silk and wool carpets, the knotting is extremely dense and they will usually last for a great many years. Wool carpets, in particular, will withstand a good deal of traffic. Some Kayseris are woven with a mercerized cotton pile that resembles silk and are produced in sizes ranging from small mats to 16 x 10ft (5 x 3m) carpets. Hereke carpets are well-known for their quality and command prices to match this. Both these areas of Turkey produce some very well-made pieces.

HOME USE

Because of the intricacy of the design and the quality of the yarn, these carpets deserve to be given a place of honour in the home. They will go well in a subtle (rather than a bold) modern scheme and are particularly suited to a dining area or living room. Smaller rugs are ideal for bedrooms.

CITY WORKSHOPS

OLD TURKISH CARPETS were woven in reds and dark and light blues, with rows of repeated lozenges, eight-pointed stars and hooked octagons. Many were woven in Ushak, which until the 16th and 17th centuries was the principal centre for the Ottoman aristocracy.

Carpet production is a relatively recent occurrence in the Hereke area in western Turkey, where carpet weaving was first introduced during the mid-19th and the beginning of the 20th centuries. It is now the source of some of Turkey's most sophisticated carpets which are distinguished by their elegance and the use of the Senneh knot, and sometimes with gold threads in the weaving of silk carpets. The style was inspired by Persian and French designs, and many follow the designs coming out of Kerman and Tabriz, while others were influenced by the Savonnerie and Aubusson carpets. Traditional Persian designs include motifs such as cloudbands, palmettes and other floral elements in a purely curvilinear style, often with a central medallion and wide borders.

The villages between the towns of Kayseri and Sivas in eastern Turkey produce short-pile rugs in a very broad range of designs, from sophisticated, curvilinear patterns influenced by those of Tabriz and Isfahan in Persia and adapted by the local Armenian weavers to much more geometric styles and prayer rugs. All these patterns are worked in the red, blue or ivory grounds that are favoured in the West. What the weavers produce is controlled nowadays by a central buying policy, so that, no matter whether the rugs are in silk or wool, they are among the finest woven today.

◁ This carpet was woven in 1992 by weavers reproducing traditional Persian designs and has the deep red field so admired in the early carpets.

△ This splendid Ushak carpet, with its enlarged floral motifs, was woven c. 1880 and would have been made specifically for the European market.

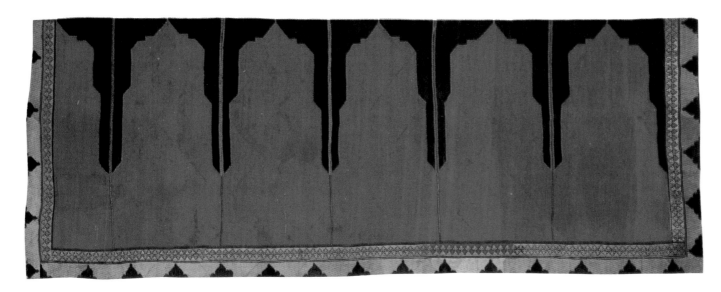

◁ A multiple prayer rug, probably woven in Ushak during the early 17th century. The simplicity of the design and the strong colours give it an almost modern appearance.

◁ A 19th-century Ushak carpet, in somewhat enlarged designs based on those of Persian carpets, on a pale ground. It has been designed with the European market in mind.

△ A rare carpet from Hereke, c. 1890, with a classic Ottoman design of tulips. It is signed "Hereke" (in bottom left corner of the picture) for the royal factory mark.

RURAL VILLAGE WEAVES

CHARACTERISTICS

Rural rugs are woven with floral patterns reminiscent of designs used in Kashan and Tabriz. Many prayer rugs are also produced, usually incorporating stylized tulips – a very popular motif among the region's weavers. Flat-weave carpets are woven in slit-weave or plain-weave, using a very broad range of designs, with dozens of motifs and a very wide colour range.

WEAR

Rural pile rugs are dense and heavy, not unlike Persian Bidjar rugs. Ladik and Konya carpets are worked in wool pile with cotton warps and wefts. Rugs from this area are becoming more expensive. Kilims are woven in standard and superior grades, and come into the medium-to-high price bracket.

HOME USE

These attractive rugs can be used in many different situations in the home, from bathroom and playroom rugs to cheerfully inviting hall rugs, on cold kitchen floors or in an informal setting in living rooms and workrooms. They will stand a good deal of wear and tear.

RURAL VILLAGE WEAVING in some areas has been very little influenced by changes in the 20th century and these communities have continued to produce tribal rugs of great integrity. Striking effects are often achieved by using blocks of colour on a white ground. Kiz carpets are tribal or village carpets that are woven by girls, with the help of their families, as part of their dowry. Traditionally, a bride would give the groom a carpet that she, herself, had made. They were intended for private family use, not for sale. These carpets can be traced back to the beginning of the 19th century and were made in a variety of designs, sometimes in a double-niche form. Natural cotton is often used to get a bright white ground, and carnations and stylized boteh motifs are also common.

Konya, a large town in central Turkey, is now a centre for workshop production although a great number of authentic regional items are still made there. It is an area of antique production of carpets and, during the 19th and into the 20th century, Konya succeeded in creating a geometric tradition of its own. Rugs are decorated with large, simple polygrams that are often stepped and hooked, and arranged in pairs or rows. Borders, decorated with a shield motif, are characteristic of the area, and are often made up of a seven- or five-sided geometric motif, again in rows, and they frequently incorporate an eight-pointed star. Nowadays, regional kilims are woven specifically for the export market.

△ A Ladik prayer rug with a triple-arched niche. The many borders contain stylized floral motifs and leaf patterns.

▷ Carpets with images of country life, like this charming modern piece, are known as folk life carpets and can be marvellously inventive and individual.

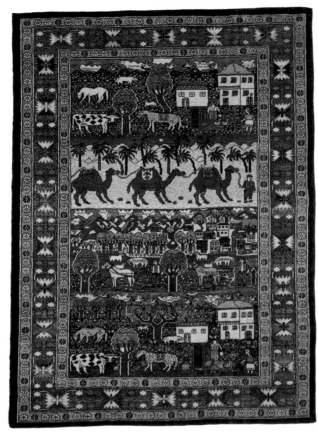

▽ This carpet is almost like a sampler, with its small squares of pattern. The bright red and blue colours are typical of Turkish rugs.

△ This prayer rug, with its central arch, has a gorgeous tree design in the centre and intricate weaving all around.

△ A modern kilim with simple motifs and bright colours, typical of the style.

WEST ANATOLIA

BERGAMA, KULA, GHIORDES and Melas are among a cluster of villages whose traditional carpets from the Classical era include large and small pattern Holbeins, carpets with double niches and prayer rugs with the typical keyhole and arrowhead designs. Melas creates some of the most authentically Anatolian items produced in the region. The most popular and distinctive design is the tree-of-life in a very stylized form and a geometric flowering diamond within a prayer rug. Melas prayer rugs have a recognizable arrowhead shape woven in warm colours. They have broad borders containing elegant, stylized floral and geometric motifs. Colours are mainly pale umber, sienna grey, rust, ochre and a greenish-yellow, which is unique to the area. Indian weavers are now copying Melas designs. Bergama designs may be either Caucasian and resemble those from Kars, a major weaving centre in the north-east of the country near the Russian border, or they may be classically Anatolian, such

CHARACTERISTICS

All the village workshops in this area today produce finely knotted carpets with woollen or cotton warps and wefts. The rugs are generally very attractive and well-made, and the dyes, whether synthetic or natural, are of good quality. The Majid style, seen in Ghiordes carpets of the mid-19th century and in Melas carpets, transformed the mihrab (niche) by filling it with realistic flowers in pastel tints.

WEAR

In some areas rugs tend to be chemically washed and bleached to achieve a paler colour, which can weaken the pile. But on the whole, these rugs are fair to medium quality and, with the strict standards imposed by the Turkish government's central buyers, they are good value for money and reasonably priced. All Kulas are in pastel shades and in the lower price range.

HOME USE

These village workshop rugs have a sophistication and robustness that makes them suitable for many uses in the home and they will brighten up a bedroom, as well as a hall. They are very versatile and will complement many different interior styles.

△ This rug, with its flower-filled columns, is one of a small group of double-ended prayer rugs from West Anatolia, made in the 17th century, of which many still survive in Eastern European churches, particularly in Transylvania.

△ Carpets from Ghiordes have always been popular in the West because of their elegant designs. They have numerous borders and the niche takes up a relatively small space.

as those woven in Melas. In Kula and Ghiordes some traditional prayer rugs are still woven, but mostly rugs have floral designs, usually with a central medallion.

Ghiordes is the best-known of Turkey's weaving centres, acclaimed for its better-than-average weaving, and it is the town that has given its name to the Turkish (symmetrical) knot. It is renowned for its marvellous prayer rugs and double-niche carpets. The area has recently introduced a broader range of Anatolian and Persian designs. Popular patterns that are woven here are naturalistic flowers, in the French style, introduced in the 1800s. Ghiordes carpets are easily recognizable because of the squat shape of the mihrab (niche) and the use of many borders.

△ An early 19th-century rug from Bergama with an Anatolian version of a garden design consisting of interlocking panels of one colour in a broad double-arrowhead formation.

◁ A modern rug in red and blue (note the abrash colour variation in the blue field) with a single medallion set in the corner.

▷ This carpet, woven in the 18th century, is similar to the large medallion Holbein rugs of the 15th, 16th and 17th centuries.

THE CAUCASUS

The Caucasus is an inaccessible mountainous region that lies between the Black Sea and the Caspian Sea, adjoining Turkey and Iran. Before it was taken over by Russia earlier on in this century, it was part of the Persian empire, but its weavers, being mountain dwellers for centuries, maintained their old traditions, using bright colours and startlingly strong geometric patterns. During the 16th and 17th centuries, the Caucasus was divided into many independent khanates (regions) that were politically tied to the Persian empire. Many of these khanates established their own carpet workshops, emulating the sophisticated city carpet workshops of Persia. Cruder versions of carpets were woven on tribal looms, producing a simplified version of the court carpet designs from memory.

Persian-type designs are still woven today, but these are now produced mainly in workshops in Armenia and Azerbaijan. Modern Caucasian rugs are woven with the Turkish (symmetrical) knot in a combination of characteristic pattern elements. Designs are much more standardized than in the older Caucasian designs and can no longer be identified with a particular region. Nowadays a rug may be called a Kazak or a Shirvan, but the name only refers to a type of pattern or colourway, not the actual place of origin.

Rugs woven in the Caucasus are usually made up of individual geometric motifs such as diapers or polygons, stars, crossed and stepped lozenges, all put together in simple, balanced juxtapositions. Hexagons, octagons and rhomboids are frequently used and, although they can be quite small, more often they are very large and can dominate the piece. Plants and animals sometimes appear and occasionally human forms, but these are always highly stylized. Designs often show the influence of motifs from Turkey and Persia.

> *Rug weaving is one of the oldest cultural traditions in the Caucasus, producing rugs that have a vivid, primitive energy and vitality. They are generally well-made with very regular knotting and good quality wool.*

THE NORTH EAST

Designs are usually of superimposed medallions or repetitions of single, small geometric motifs over the whole field. Popular motifs include the serrated leaf, running dog, geometric vine, various type of polygon, ram's horn, cross and anchor, eagle or adler medallion and cloudband medallion. Many carpets have an arrangement of medallions along a central axis. Caucasian prayer rugs can be recognized by a tiny geometric arch at the top of the design. Caucasian carpet designs are widely copied in India and Pakistan, often in a finer weave than the originals and with modified colours.

WEAR

Pile rugs from the Caucasus reproduce the older regional styles exactly and are made in superior quality, with excellent weaving with a cotton warp and weft (no longer wool as in the past). The pile is trimmed to medium height.

HOME USE

These rugs are very strong, both in quality and in design. They can be used absolutely anywhere in the house, but they do require an environment that can match the strength of the motifs. A medallion rug in ivory on a dark red or blue ground is as strong as a modern sculpture and will detract from other decoration unless carefully placed.

CAUCASIAN RUGS COME in a wide range of colours and geometric designs, with blue and red for backgrounds. A rug may be called a Shirvan, but the name only refers to the pattern. Ancient Caucasian populations probably learned the technique of knotting from the Seljuk invaders in the 11th century, but nothing survives from that time – not even any pictures – and the oldest known examples of carpets date from the 16th and 17th centuries, by which time Persian influences were much in evidence.

Russian rule in the early 19th century meant the end of the nobility and, therefore, the decline of the specialized workshops and the Persian influence. This gave an opportunity for the small village workshops to come to the fore and there was then a period of discovery of traditional motifs and techniques, going back to early weaving roots, and perhaps even to the early Seljuk traditions, but the court motifs were absorbed into these designs and these are the carpets that are found today.

Caucasian rugs are lively, abstract, bold and noticeable. Shirvan come in three basic designs: large medallions (with the open spaces filled with small motifs), overall patterns of tiny, geometric floral motifs and prayer rugs with blue and ivory ground. Baku carpets have large motifs and muted colours such as ivory, blue and light blue. They are woven in small, neat individual geometric motifs and in the floral and boteh forms. Striped medallions, which originally come from Iran, are more in evidence than in rugs that are woven in other areas. Hila (Chila) carpets have a medallion layout with corner motifs and the field is closely covered with botehs. Kuba carpets are very similar to Bakus, but the pile is longer and the colours much brighter. In the mountainous area of Daghestan, coarse carpets with a high pile are woven.

◁ Geometric medallions, superimposed one on another, characterize this Shirvan carpet. Typically, each medallion is joined to the next by a narrow segment and the borders have a design of hooked triangles.

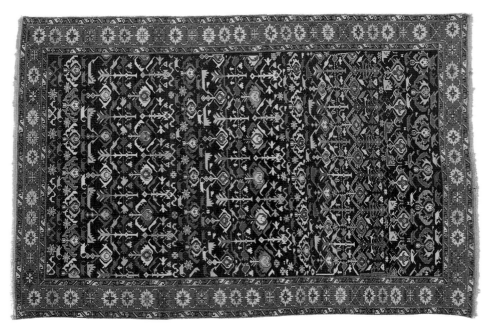

◁ A Kuba rug
with a lively
design of stylized
pomegranates and
leaves in red, dark
and pale blue, and
sandy outlines.

△ A Kuba runner with a colourful
field and a typical border of
repeated geometric motifs.

▷ An attractive, geometric
carpet from Daghestan with
a notched grid containing
stylized floral elements.

△ This small rug has a ram's horn motif in
the corners, outlined in white, which is often
found in carpets from the area of Kuba.

65

CHARACTERISTICS

These carpets have a definite Persian influence in the designs. Dragon and floral carpets are typical of those woven during the 16th and 17th centuries. Many auctions of oriental rugs today include several lots of these old imports, which can be very good buys. So-called "Classical rugs", made before 1800, still come up for sale from time to time.

WEAR

Old rugs are often in poor condition and require cleaning and conserving. They should be hung on a wall, out of direct sunlight, if they are to last. However, modern carpets in the same style are made of good quality wool and these are perfectly robust and should last for many years.

HOME USE

Old Caucasian rugs in good condition can fetch extremely high prices, but many interesting old examples in a poorer condition can be found in auctions for reasonable prices and, when cleaned, repaired and mounted, these precious old pieces can look very handsome hung on a wall. Modern versions are also very attractive and can be used in the reception rooms of the home to good effect.

PERSIAN DESIGNS

DURING THE 16TH and 17th centuries, the Caucasus came under Persian rule and carpets that were woven in important workshops during this period display all the characteristics of Persian weaving, in both structure and design. They reached their peak in the 19th century, when small, thickly piled and brilliantly coloured rugs became fashionable in the West; a hundred years ago they were the most popular of all oriental rugs and a great many of them found their way to Europe. The influence of Persia can be seen particularly in dragon and floral carpets, which have borrowed the Persian floral and curvilinear style.

Dragon carpets consist of small dragon motifs, spread within narrow, stylized leaves over the whole field. The motifs are so highly stylized as to be more or less unrecognizable. Floral carpets have overall patterns of small medallions and palmettes. Both these types of carpet were woven in specialist workshops for wealthy clients. The older, regional styles are still made today – with a great deal of integrity – and they are of superior quality. Nineteenth-century carpets were made by a number of workshops (and in many diverse patterns) but with very characteristic colours, such as a glowing pinky violet and a variety of greens and yellows.

△ This early 17th-century, wonderfully bold carpet probably comes from Kuba. Although it has much of the characteristic Caucasian boldness of motif, the influence of Persian carpets can be seen in the detail of the motifs, including the cloudbands in the ivory panel.

◁ A rare carpet, with horsemen, animals and flowers, and a medallion and cartouche border, that was woven in the late 18th century, based on Safavid Persian hunting carpets of the 16th and 17th centuries.

▽ This beautiful late 17th-century dragon carpet is a museum piece and shows a strong Persian influence in its design.

△ Karabagh carpets are made in many different styles, from traditional village designs to those based on Persian and European designs. This one has a floral motif in the borders and stripes based on traditional Persian embroidery designs.

▷ Shirvan carpets are characterized by small, decorated elements, arranged very close together. In this prayer rug, a definite Persian influence can be seen.

KAZAK

CHARACTERISTICS

Easily recognized by the few but prominent main decorative elements which dominate the designs. They are geometric in style and may be octagons, hexagons, swastikas, eight-pointed stars or rectangles.

WEAR

These are good, medium-quality rugs. Unfortunately, they are being made in fewer and fewer quantities and, even when they are available, Kazaks are likely to be fairly small in size. The largest Kazak is generally about 10 x 7ft (3 x 2m).

HOME USE

These rugs are bold and dramatic, so they should be placed where they will not dominate or detract from a subtle interior scheme. They look great in dining rooms, kitchens and halls.

KAZAK IS THE NAME given to rugs from the west and south-west of the Caucasus that boast of large, relatively simple, geometric designs in sharply contrasting colours, usually bright reds, greens and yellows. Bold decorative motifs and bright, clean colours are typical of 19th-century Kazak rugs. The main border design often includes stylized tulips against a lighter background. Colours are rich but muted when compared with modern examples. Nevertheless, the geometric medallions, so confident and bold, still stand out joyfully. The medallion itself is often in ivory or pale yellow on a very rich, deep background. These medallions often take up a large part of the centre of the carpet – there may only be room for one or two and may be arranged in a row along the central axis. The medallions are often hooked. Sometimes they are in the form of a large, centralized motif, similar to a butterfly or shield. These are sometimes called Sevan, after the area of production. Designs include snake-like patterns, cloudbands and crests. The pile is relatively thick but now, like much of the weaving carried out in the region, the warp and weft are often in cotton, rather than in the traditional wool.

One well-known form of Kazak is made up of three cruciform medallions in blue or green, with extending rays. Each is surrounded by a thick, white line and the centre is a smaller medallion against a red background. These are usually accompanied by stylized geometric decorations spread against a red field. The medallions are based on antique floral motifs and have been devised by taking a motif and enlarging it, then using it in new ways. These are known as eagle or adler Kazaks or Chelberds, from the town of Chelabi in the Karabagh region, where they are supposed to have been woven. Copies of the classic Kazak patterns are now being woven in Turkey (Anatolia), particularly in Dosemealti, and in Romania. Other adaptations are being made in India.

△ This cloudband-patterned rug, in its bold colours and strong design, is typical of old carpets from Kazak.

▽ A Kazak rug, woven in the 19th century, is easily recognized by its imposing, large medallions which dominate the design and the strong, brilliant colours.

△ Sometimes called an eagle/adler Kazak or a Chelberd, this rug features a magnificent sunburst design, based on a 17th-century Persian motif which has been adapted into a distinctive Caucasian design.

△ This Kazak prayer rug, with medallions, abstract elements and the pentagonal form of niche, is typical of a type known as fachralo.

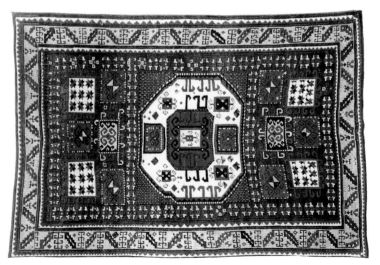

◁ This carpet is dominated by a central octagonal medallion in brilliant white, with characteristic hook motifs and a border of serrated leaves.

FLAT-WEAVES

CAUCASIAN KILIMS, woven in the 18th, 19th and early 20th centuries before the country became part of the Soviet Union, were among the finest ever woven. Today, these kilims are keenly sought after by collectors and they do still come onto the market from time to time. Several different techniques are used throughout the Caucasus to weave kilims, including slit-weave, plain-weave and supplementary weft techniques, such as zilli and verneh.

Soumak is a comparatively rare type of kilim, deriving its name from the old town of Shemakja. Caucasian soumaks are a durable, often delicately patterned rug.

Verneh is the name given to a group of old Caucasian kilims, which were produced until the mid-20th century, using the soumak technique (a kind of herringbone stitch which is embroidered in a loosely woven plain weave). Vernehs were made in deep reds, blues and whites. Shahsavan weavers produce similar items, but the older ones are much more desirable than these. Cotton flat-weaves are also made. Antique soumaks, dating back to the early 19th century, use typically rusty brown colours and feature geometric motifs, which are taken from those used in Caucasian pile rugs. The most popular patterns include medallions, the running dog

CHARACTERISTICS

Caucasian kilims show, with certain common features, the varied influences of the Kurdish, Anatolian and Persian cultures. The basic structure is wool and the white designs are often highlighted with undyed cotton. Designs are mostly repeated patterns of geometric motifs, usually saw-toothed medallions arranged in rows. They are generally marketed (like pile rugs) under the names of traditional weaving groups such as Shirvan. Flat-weaves are still widely available and they make excellent furnishing items.

WEAR

Workshop kilims are generally of good quality and they are produced in a range of traditional designs but lack the individuality and subtlety that characterize traditional kilim weaving in the Caucasus. Kilims from Armenia and Azerbaijan are more like traditional Caucasian kilims than the workshop ones. They are comparatively scarce and are entirely made of wool with elongated format and are both compact and strong.

HOME USE

Caucasian flat-weaves, with their strong patterns and colours, will make a splendid statement in a large space. They look particularly good on polished wood floors or ceramic tiles. Strong daylight or a daylight bulb will bring out their marvellous colours.

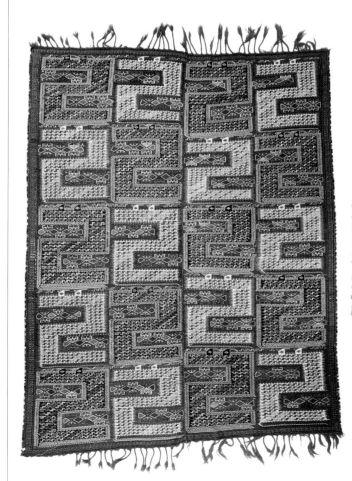

◁ This 19th-century brocaded soumak has a distinctive design which, when looked at horizontally, seems to represent a caravan of camels.

△ This is a typical soumak, with central medallions, geometric designs, narrow borders and rich colours ranging between rust and rose.

and eight-pointed stars. Large Caucasian kilims also use the stylized dragon motif.

Azerbaijan regional kilims evolved from traditional pile rugs woven in Kuba, Gendje and Kazak. A number of weaving techniques are used that are similar to Armenian techniques, but the rugs are more Islamic in character and style. They are very similar to items woven by ethnic Azerbaijanis in Iran. Azerbaijan is the largest producer of kilims in the region.

Daghestan regional kilims are known locally as davaghins. They often have deep blue fields decorated with complex medallions in deep, rusty brown. Again, they are frequently woven in soumak, slit-weave or plain-weave techniques. Traditional Caucasian designs are still used in today's workshops.

During the Soviet period, traditional kilims were woven for both domestic purposes and for export to the West. Most of those that were woven for export were produced in workshops.

Armenian kilims are well-made and based on traditional Caucasian rugs, including those made in Nagorny, Karabagh and Azerbaijan. They are known locally as "karpets".

▷ A kilim with small, overall medallions and a primitive, geometric quality. The white border provides an effective framework for the busy centre field.

▽ This traditional verneh was woven using soumak supplementary weft techniques and typical geometric motifs in relatively subdued colours.

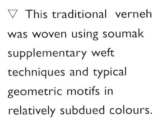

△ This pretty, small soumak has one very ornate medallion with abstract motifs, a narrow border with rows of rosettes and lively colours.

CENTRAL ASIA

In the context of carpet making, Central Asia is a vast area that includes West Turkestan (now Afghanistan), East Turkestan (bordering onto China and the former Soviet republics of Turkmenistan, Uzbekhistan and Tadzhakistan), Kirghistan and south Kazakhstan. It lies between Siberia to the north, Tibet and India to the south and the Caspian Sea to the west. This is an arid land of several million square miles, largely inhabited by semi-nomadic tribes of Turkoman origin, including Uighur, Tadzhik, Uzbek, Kazak and Kirghiz tribespeople, as well as Mongolians and Chinese.

For over 2,000 years, the Turkoman nomads have tended flocks and woven rugs and blankets for their own use. At the beginning of the 20th century they split, with Russia in the west and China in the east. In the western regions of this area, Afghanistan and West Turkestan, the designs and motifs of the rugs have been influenced by Iran and Islam, while in the eastern part,

The influence of both China and Persia can clearly be seen in the carpets produced by the weavers of Central Asia. In the east of the region, Chinese colours are used; in the west, Persian colours predominate.

East Turkestan and Tibet have been much more influenced by China.

Ornamental carpets, with animal patterns and fragments, have been found in Central Asia, Egypt and West Turkestan and these were influenced by Persian and Islamic motifs. The Persian-influenced rugs produced by nomadic village and workshop looms are almost always in red, with a pattern usually based on a repeat gul pattern or vegetal motifs. Most of the rugs that have been woven in the east of the region have similar designs and motifs as in the western region. However, the details and infill decorations are definitely Chinese in colour and feeling. In the west of the region, deep blues and reds predominate; in the eastern part colours are softer and tend towards oranges, yellows and blues. Persian and Chinese influences seem to meet more or less in a line from north to south, from Kashgar to Delhi. This combination of influences has helped to create a wonderful variety of colours, motifs and designs.

EAST TURKESTAN

Strong Chinese and Mogul influences can be seen in 17th- and 18th-century weavings from Yarkand, Kashgar and Khotan. They are expensive and rarely available. Characteristic motifs include pomegranates, multiple saph designs, lattice and peony motifs.

WEAR

Although workshop-made, 19th- and early 20th-century examples retain many of the qualities of early nomadic weaving, from which they are derived. They are well-made in long-lasting materials. Often wool is the only yarn used in their production, although nowadays cotton may be used for the warps and weft.

HOME USE

These attractive rugs (which are often larger than the traditional nomadic pieces) can be used as hangings, floor coverings, bed coverings or what you will. Their traditional deep reds are very attractive in many colour schemes, although they would not look their best in pastel, "frilly" interiors.

WHEN SAMARKAND AND Tashkent became incorporated into the USSR, the three weaving towns of Kashgar, Yarkand and Khotan became part of the People's Republic of China. Their names are now used to classify East Turkestan carpets, but the rugs which come from these towns are not very different in style or technique from those woven elsewhere, so they can be difficult to identify. In addition, it is hardly possible to tell whether a rug is more characteristic of one town than another and pomegranate designs or the central gul medallion may come from any or all of the three towns and some of the rugs that use this design were probably woven in China. Traditionally, Khotan is associated with saph designs (multiple prayer rugs where two or more niches lie alongside each other in one rug), similar to those woven in Kayseri, Turkey. Silk rugs, too, are thought to be more likely to come from the Khotan region.

Yarkand is often associated with pomegranate and medallion motifs. Some experts consider Yarkand rugs to be woven with a slightly different technique to other East Turkestan rugs, but this has not been proven. Kashgar is also associated with pomegranate schemes, especially those with a rather fine latticing motif, and peony medallions and other floral and lattice designs. Rugs that are not given the name of one of these three regions are normally sold as East Turkestan rugs.

Samarkand was a commercial centre for the products woven in the area, particularly those made in East and Chinese Turkestan. They were colourful, combining Turkoman designs with Chinese colours, and became collectively known as Samarkands. Old Samarkands are extremely rare and valuable. Contemporary Samarkands are workshop versions of old rugs from Khotan, Kashgar, Yarkand and other East Turkestan rugs.

△ This antique Khotan carpet is similar to Bokhara and Beshir rugs to look at, but has larger motifs and more pastel shades.

◁ A Khotan or Samarkand rug with a pale field and large floating blue floral motifs leading from a blue vase at either end.

▷ This East Turkestan rug has blue, floral motifs on a dark field with a wide border of what is almost a cloudband pattern.

◁ This rug shows influences from the West its border of serrated leaves. The round medallions and pale colour are indicative of Chinese influences.

TURKOMAN WEAVES

Small, balanced overall motifs (in particular, the gul motif) appear not only on rugs but also on many artefacts used in the nomadic lifestyle, including bags for clothes, bedding and foods, animal trappings, gun covers, hangings, floor coverings and wedding items (which are among the finest weavings available). Contemporary examples are woven in workshops over a wide area from Afghanistan to East Turkestan, and their colour is predominantly red.

WEAR

These are tough and durable items, made to be used, and they should last a very long time, whether they are intended to be walked upon or enjoyed in some other way. Wool is used in the foundation materials as well as for the pile. Modern factory-produced rugs are made in a greater range of sizes than their smaller, nomadic counterparts.

HOME USE

Many of the smaller items can be used as they were intended: for carrying and storing household items. Sometimes a bag or trapping can be opened out and turned into a small rug or hanging. Double bags can be hung over the arms of a chair to hold magazines or knitting.

TURKOMAN IS THE generic name given to geometric, repeating designs that were originally woven by Turkmen, who are among the most outstanding groups of nomadic weaving tribes in Central Asia. In the late 19th century, many Turkmen tribespeople fled to Afghanistan. Carpets made before the migration have a wide range of colours and are often based on the so-called elephant gul motifs that can be seen in later Afghan rugs. Turkmen weavers work on small looms, so they nearly always use small motifs which they balance in each piece as they wish.

One of the important features of tribal carpets and weaving is that the colours are not uniform. There are innumerable shades of the same colour, known as abrashes. This is a feature of natural dyes and gives a liveliness and interest which cannot be obtained with machine-spun yarns and chemical dyes.

Bokhara was on the first silk route from China and originally, the name Bokhara applied to any rug that was marketed in the town. The Salor, Chodor, Ersari, Yomut, Saryk and Tekke were the main tribes in the region

producing weavings, and they still do so. The Belouch nomads on the borderland of Iran and Afghanistan are often included in the general Turkmen group, but their rugs do have special characteristics of their own.

Bokhara carpets are always in deep shades of red, with repeating patterns of octagonal gul motifs in dark blue, black or brown and white accents. In early pieces, there are subtle differences in technique, ornaments and colouring from one tribe to another, and these differences are the traditional means of identifying some of the origins of a rug. Today, the term Bokhara refers only to contemporary rugs employing the traditional gul motif.

Bokharas are nowadays mainly produced in commercial workshops. Russian Turkmens are usually marketed as Bokharas or Beshirs, depending on their design. Those made in Afghanistan are generally known as Afghans or Bokharas. Bokhara carpets made in Afghanistan are thicker and heavier, with a velvet-like surface and the warm red colour of many Afghan carpets. They are regarded in the trade as high-quality Afghans

◁ A Beshir rug in typical Turkoman deep reds and blues, but enlivened by paler shades in the narrow border.

and are referred to as dowlatabads, from the town in which they are made. Contemporary Afghans, together with Bokhara and Beshir, are major sources of the famous red carpets of Central Asia. Originally woven almost entirely by nomadic groups, today they are also made in villages and workshops. Wherever they are made, they retain the same designs, motifs, colours and general characteristics as the tribal originals.

A less common type of rug from Central Asia is the Beshir, which has wool warps and medium-cut pile. These rugs are unusual in that they are often given geometric designs other than the more usual gul generally seen in Turkoman weaving. Beshir rugs are usually very finely woven and have rather crowded fields, often worked in stylized floral patterns. They are produced in fairly small room sizes. Beshir are made in both Turkmenistan and Afghanistan. The designs are usually very repetitive and borders are formed by many narrow bands in alternating colours. These are usually worked on fields of dark blue, with the design itself in shades of red with distinctive yellow accents.

Nowadays, large numbers of rugs in Bokhara and Beshir designs are produced in Pakistan and India.

▷ A Turkoman bride rides to her wedding in a covered litter, on a camel decorated with trappings made by herself and her family for the occasion. Wedding trappings are woven with the best materials, often including silk, and the greastest skill, and they are among the finest Turkoman weavings to be found. Pictured top and bottom are a pair of torbas (storage bags) woven by the Tekke and Ersari tribes respectively. In the centre are two camel trappings, the rectangular one woven by the Saryk tribe. The other is an asmalyk, a twin-flank trapping used to adorn the bridal litter, woven by the Yomut tribe.

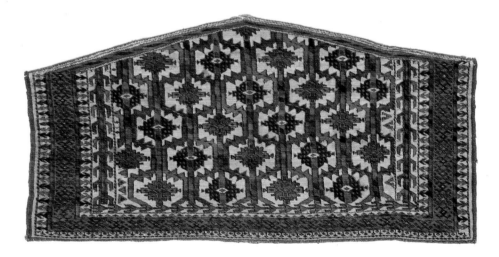

▷ This Bokhara carpet, woven in Afghanistan by the Ersari tribe in rich reds, blue and white, may have started life as a door hanging. The four-square design, each segment decorated with the same pattern, is known as hatchli.

△ This fine Bokhara carpet is woven in a sophisticated design of red pomegranates on an intricate floral background. The border contains the same pattern.

▷ This very rare carpet, woven by the Tekke tribe, has a typical arrangement of Tekke guls in offset rows of major and minor guls.

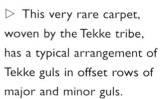

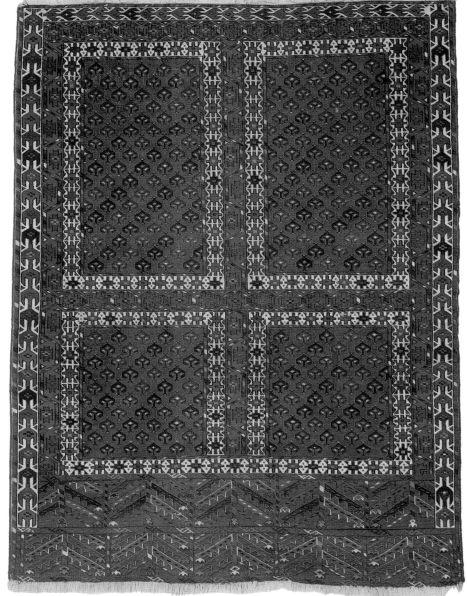

◁ An attractive and sturdy Beshir prayer rug in a traditional design. Typically, it is less deeply red than many Bokharas and is enlivened by paler shades with a distinctive central pattern.

▷ An asymmetrical Yomut flat-weave, with an all-over gul design in typical brownish-red colours, and with geometric patterns and white outlines.

INDIA & PAKISTAN

Indian carpet making first appeared as an art form during the Mogul dynasty when Akbar, the Mogul ruler from 1556–1605, set up workshops in Agra, Fatehpur Sikri and Lahore, with artists and weavers from the Persian court. Originally, carpets were woven to Safavid Persian court designs, but soon the Mogul court designers developed a distinctive style of their own and these designs have remained influential to this day.

Carpet making was introduced in India and Pakistan by the Moguls, who set up royal workshops employing weavers from Persia. Soon, however, Mogul court designers developed their own unique style.

Some of the carpets from the 17th century are among the greatest examples of hand-knotted carpets ever made. They had a foundation of silk, pile of Kashmiri goat and an enormous number of knots to the square inch. Almost all of them are now in museum collections. Classical Indian carpets are characterized by yellow, pink, light blue and green colours and lac red, which is used only for grounds of fields. All Indian carpets are made

Weaving has always taken place in urban workshops only. Rug weaving practically died out soon after the Mogul period and was only revived when, in the mid-1800s, the British government introduced it into prisons as a commercial venture. "Jail carpets", as they are known, are often copies of Safavid Persian rugs and are very collectible (and therefore expensive) today.

with the Senneh (asymmetrical) knot and the pile is usually trimmed low. In contemporary Indian and Pakistani workshops, weavers use a talim, a written-out pattern which records every knot of a pattern onto paper as a sequence of signs. The instructions are often read out by a caller in a rhythmic chanting of the sequence and number of knots and colours to the weavers.

CARPETS AND DHURRIES

THE DHURRIE IS the Indian equivalent of the kilim, in that it is woven using the flat-weave technique, but the dhurrie is essentially a cotton rug, whereas kilims are nearly always woven in wool. The cotton gives them a solid, heavy quality that is characteristic of that particular yarn. Traditionally, dhurries were woven in a tremendous range of qualities, colours, sizes and designs, and each had a specific function. At its most basic, the dhurrie is a huge, coarse, thick, striped object: the "bed-size" dhurrie, which acts as a sort of futon-type mattress. Another type of dhurrie was woven as a prayer rug, often in the form of a multiple niche or saph with mihrab arch, rosettes and other symbols. The Hindus often wove individual dhurries called asans. Room or palace pieces may be very large indeed and these are only made to specific orders for use at weddings and other festivals. Special dhurries, made in the Deccan and Rajasthan, are constructed with cotton warps and silk wefts, and some have cotton warps and wool wefts. They should not be confused with a class of Indian flat-weaves called druggets, which have cotton warp and poor-quality wool wefts.

CHARACTERISTICS

In Pakistan and Kashmir, workshop carpets are produced in old carpet designs, in both wool and silk. They are intricate, curvilinear and often pictorial. Kashmir carpets are often woven in brighter colours than those woven in Pakistan. Dhurries are flat-woven, usually small, cotton rugs, in a variety of geometric motifs and designs and a wide range of pastel colours.

WEAR

The Kashmir area is noted for its silk carpets, which generally come in a wide range of sizes. All will give many years of wear. Dhurries are tough and durable. To gauge the quality of a dhurrie, count the number of warps and rows of wefts and compare them with the count of similar pieces.

HOME USE

Workshop carpets have a very glossy appearance and would look good in a bedroom. Smaller rugs could give as much pleasure as bedside rugs. Dhurries are highly attractive and can be used in all areas of the home. The darker ones are good in heavy traffic areas, whereas the paler ones look very good in the modern, small living room and are eminently suitable for children's rooms.

△ This carpet, woven around 1890, is inspired by a classical 17th-century Persian design that has been enlarged to create a more forceful pattern.

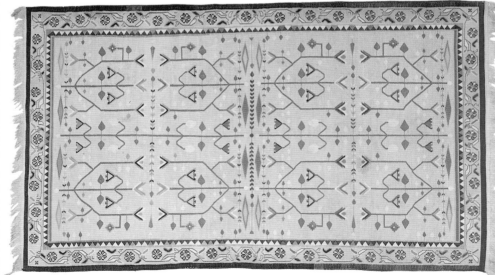

◁ A meticulously woven dhurrie. Its long, narrow leaf stalks and flower outlines would have taken time and patience to weave.

▷ A modern tree carpet woven from hand-spun wool. The wool has been dyed using plants such as pomegranate, henna, madder and indigo.

▽ An Indo-Persian garden carpet with the narrow water channels, central pool, shady trees and secluded gardens beloved by both the Persian and Mogul emperors.

Dhurries are now woven in workshops throughout India and, to a lesser extent, Pakistan, and a new generation of dhurries has appeared, designed with the Western market very much in mind. These new dhurries, with their cheerful, pastel colours, excellent weaving and quality are now widely available at very reasonable prices.

A number of other carpet types are also made in workshops in Kashmir and Uttar Pradesh using Persian-inspired medallion, vase, paradise, prayer rug, panelled garden and all-over floral designs. The colours of Kashmir carpets are less pastel than other Indian and Pakistani weaving, but paler than most Persian rugs. Kashmir carpets may be made using the lagri knot (the Indian equivalent of the Persian jufti knot). This knot is quicker to work but not so meticulous, so it is important to inspect a carpet carefully before buying. Excellent carpets are also being produced in nearby Nepal in comparatively recently established workshops employing Tibetan refugees. They are sometimes marketed as kangris and a number of other names may be used.

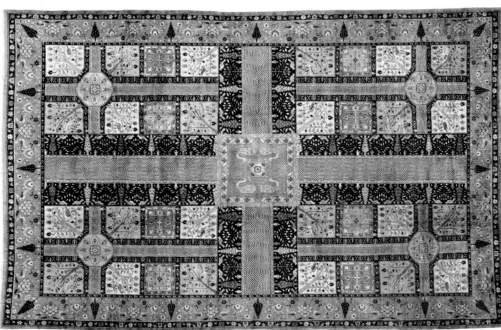

△ A modern Indian folk rug, similar in spirit to Turkish folklife carpets. It depicts temples and mosques, motor rickshaws and other aspects of everyday village life.

◁ An unusually fine modern
dhurrie with a plain, dark blue
centre and floral and wavy borders.
It was woven just outside Delhi.

▷ A rare Mogul prayer rug with
large, flowering chrysanthemums.
It dates back to the late 17th or
early 18th century.

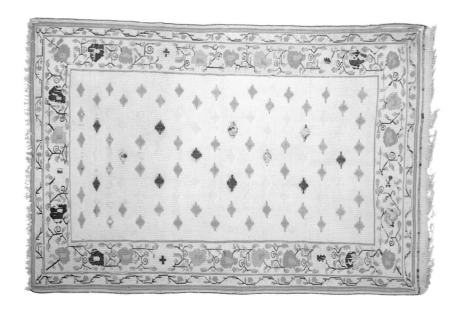

◁ A fine, old dhurrie with a field of repeated small diamonds and intricate, curvilinear floral motifs in the border.

◁ A modern carpet in a traditional design using natural dyes and hand-spun wool. It has an attractive abrash effect.

△ A contemporary carpet, based on an old Indian design, with a central medallion and intricate field and borders.

CHARACTERISTICS

Antique carpets, woven in jails across India and Pakistan in the 19th century and up to the First World War. In mostly traditional designs, they feature excellent quality weaving.

WEAR

These are historic rugs and, if they do come onto the market, they should be tenderly cared for. They are extremely fine, with rows of very tight and fine yarns and knotting with excellent wearing qualities. They are much sought after and can therefore be quite expensive.

HOME USE

These carpets are tough, hard-wearing and very sound furnishing carpets. They also look beautiful as wall hangings.

JAIL CARPETS

AS THE MOGUL empire declined, so did the production of hand-knotted carpets in royal workshops, which seems to have come to an end by the beginning of the 19th century. There was little indigenous tradition of weaving when the royal carpets ceased to be produced and so carpet weaving virtually died out. However, during the second half of the 19th century, weaving was encouraged by the British government and weaving groups were established in privately owned factories, villages and various orphanages, charitable institutions and missionary schools. Government-controlled production of both hand-knotted rugs and flat-woven dhurries was encouraged in jails all over the country. The Crystal Palace Exhibition in London in 1851 excited a new interest in carpets woven throughout the Indian sub-continent and, as a result, the Indian carpet trade was revived. From the 1860s, the industry grew apace and had reached its peak by the early 1890s.

Many more dhurries than pile carpets were woven because they were easier, quicker and cheaper to produce. Selected inmates were trained in flat-weaving, but pile-knotting was usually done by those inmates who were already experienced weavers and then only to special commission. Weavers either wove directly from examples that were on loan to the jail or they adapted designs from book illustrations. Patterns travelled around from jail to jail and Indo-Persian, Herat and Isfahan designs were all woven. The jails in Lahore, Agra and Montgomery produced some of the finest carpets, while other carpet-producing jails included Hyderabad and Ahmedabad.

◁ An Agra carpet, typical of the sophisticated designs made in many of the jails in India and Pakistan during the 19th century.

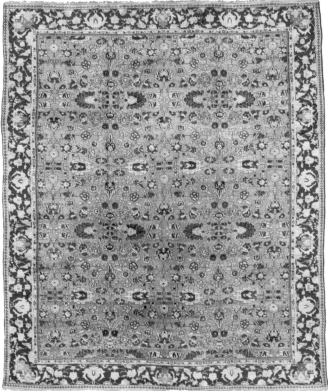

◁△ A handsome floral carpet of Indo-Isfahan design, woven *c.* 1880 in Agra, with the curvilinear motifs typical of Persian-influenced jail carpets.

◁ The wide border of floral medallions on a rich red ground exemplifies the Persian influences on the designs produced in the jails of India and Pakistan.

△ A large carpet with intertwining floral festoons on a deep red field and pomegranate and other floral motifs. It is based on Caucasian dragon carpets.

NORTH AFRICA

Carpets from Egypt and other important North African weaving countries (mainly Morocco, but also Algeria and Tunisia) are classified as Mediterranean. Early carpets from Spain are often classified as Mediterranean too and, in many ways, have more in common with those from North Africa than with other European weavings. North Africa also has several minor rug-weaving countries that have not really found favour in the West.

Egyptian weaving goes back to pre-history and a few Mamluk pile carpets from the 15th and early 16th centuries are still to be found in museums today. Mamluk carpet designs are geometric, but they often have intricate and meticulous infill motifs and patterns. The influence of Ottoman rule (early 16th to late 18th century) gradually changed the geometric to something more curvilinear and some of the Ottoman court carpets are among the finest examples of Egyptian work. The

African weaving dates back to the ancient Egyptians. Today, kilims are made by many tribes throughout North Africa as well as in contemporary workshops. Morocco is the biggest producer of these rugs.

18th century saw a decline in Egyptian carpet weaving, but during the last 20 to 30 years they have begun to produce reproductions for the decorative market. Today the Cairo area produces some of the best quality reproduction items in the world, in both wool and silk. They are made in a number of Persian workshop designs, although other designs can be found too.

Morocco, Algeria and Tunisia produce a range of attractive tribal and nomadic items but they also make products of poorer (and often garish) quality for the tourist market in local bazaars. Several Berber and Bedouin tribespeople throughout North Africa produce attractive, brightly coloured rugs in predominantly geometric designs that have been influenced by rugs from Anatolia, Persia and Central Asia. Rugs in mainly brown and grey shades of undyed wool are also woven. They are, in general, well made with a sturdy, primitive quality.

MOROCCO

MOROCCO IS A constitutional monarchy with a population of mainly Arab people but there are also many Berbers, Kurds and Persians. Berbers were the original inhabitants, but the country was occupied by the Romans and the Carthaginians for relatively short periods and then it was invaded in the 7th century by the Arabs, who became the major ethnic group. Spain and France ruled different parts of the country during the 19th and early 20th centuries, but in 1956 Morocco became an independent country. Moroccan kilims are produced by tribal, regional and contemporary workshop weaving groups and Morocco is the largest exporter of kilims from north Africa, although there are a number of ethnic weaving groups in Algeria and Tunisia, and Berber influence is very much in evidence in regional and workshop items throughout the area. The pieces are generally of good quality and attractive.

Today the best authentic weaving in Morocco is produced by nomadic, semi-nomadic or settled weavers in the Tennsift coastal region, and in the High and Middle Atlas mountain ranges by weaving groups that include Berber, Azrou Boujaad, Hanbel, Oudzem Taznakht and Tiffelt. Individual tribes each create their own particular rug designs, primarily for domestic use or to sell at local markets, and only a few of the larger groups produce enough work to make a significant impact on the Western market.

Middle Atlas tribal weavings include Beni M'Guild kilims, which are usually fairly large with decorated bands and square compartments in dark colours with white outlines. Beni M'Tir kilims are similar, but these are often made up of repeating diamonds. Ben Quarain kilims are small to medium size, often in alternating stripes of single colours with highly intricate, weft-faced patterning in contrasting colours. Zain and Zaiane kilims are similar and available in a variety of sizes using dark colours. Zemmour are mainly large and often in bright colours on a pale red ground.

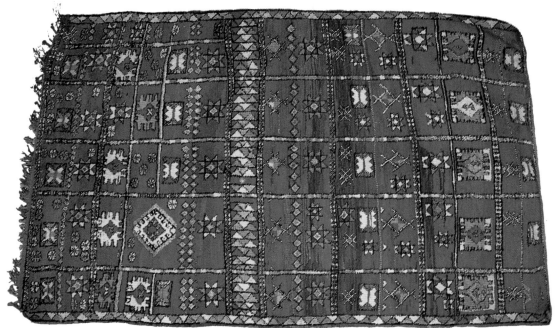

▷ A large, rectangular kilim from the western Middle Atlas meseta. It has been woven by the Zemmour c. 1870–1880 and has a very bright palette. The Zemmour tribe is one of the most prolific of the Berber weaving groups.

△ This interesting grey and pink rug in zigzag stripes was woven by the Beni M'Guild tribe in the Middle Atlas mountains. It dates back to the late 19th or early 20th century.

▷ This rug, in hot orange and yellow, was woven by the Rehamna M'zil tribe in Marrakech in the mid-20th century. It has a small diamond medallion and narrow stripes.

◁ The meticulous, intricate weaving in this bright yellow and red rug was produced by the Zemmour tribe during the first half of the 20th century.

▷ This kilim, in a lattice design with tiny floral motifs inside, changes from sand to a wonderful sunset colour. It was woven by the Aït Ouaouzguit tribe in southern Morocco in the mid-20th century.

▽ A bright red kilim in a finely executed, almost lace-like pattern interspersed with tiny floral motifs. It has been woven by the Boujaad tribe of central western Morocco in the mid-20th century.

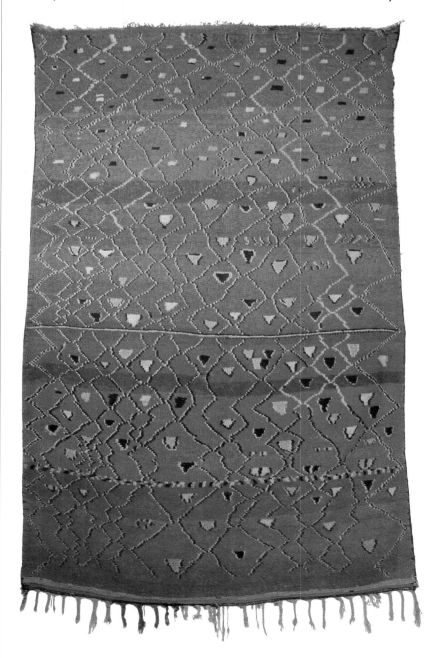

▽ North African kilim, typically arranged in rows. It is densely filled with items of interest: squares filled with diamonds, serrated leaves and a convoy of camels.

◁ This rug, with its bright red ground and joyful scattering of diamond-shaped and other motifs, was woven by the Rehamna Ould D'lim tribe in Marrakech in the mid-20th century.

CHINA & TIBET

A few main weaving centres in China itself have given their names to styles of carpet. Important centres were Peking, Tientsin, Suiyan and Kansu. Tientsin workshops made rugs whose main markets were North America and Europe. They were cheap, handmade and concentrated on more Western colours and designs. Motifs were flowers, birds, trees, vases, boats and pagodas in naturalistic mode, and predominant colours were burgundy, burnt orange, green, purple, mauve and turquoise.

Suiyan and Kansu, on the borders of lower Mongolia, produced fairly small rugs with thick pile and designs are usually in various shades of blue. Motifs include medallions with frets, peonies, swastikas and other geometric emblems, plus a horse or deer under a tree.

There are references to rugs in China during the Tang dynasty (AD 618–907), but most surviving old rugs date from the 17th to 19th centuries. Tibetans carpets include "tiger rugs" and simple geometric designs.

Contemporary rugs are made to traditional designs. Kansu designs are usually in blues and whites with small amounts of extra colour. The area of southern Tibet, known as Dampa Dzong, produces wool carpets that are coarsely knotted, in relatively simple geometric designs – a cheerful form of peasant weaving that is very attractive.

During the communist years, the idea was to produce cheap, decent quality rugs for a broad range of Western tastes that were based on the ideas of Peking and Tientsin. After the Revolution, four ranges of styles of rugs were developed, which became known as Aesthetic (Aubusson designs, for example), Peking (traditional), Floral and Self-tone (embossed or sculptured), all loosely based on concepts produced in the Peking and Tientsin workshops at the beginning of this century.

NINGXIA, PEKING & TIBET

CHARACTERISTICS

Classic Chinese carpets usually contain a central medallion in an open field. Motifs are either familiar objects seen in nature or stylized Chinese ideographs. Care should be taken in trying to identify a carpet by its motifs as almost identical designs can be found in rugs from a number of different weaving areas.

WEAR

All Chinese rugs are woven in government-run workshops and each centre has its own colour and design preferences, but the strict quality controls mean that all carpets are of the same quality. They use excellent materials and their rugs usually keep their fine appearance after years of use. The materials, whether wool, goat hair or silk, are all dyed with Chinese dyes.

HOME USE

These carpets use excellent materials and usually maintain their fine appearance after several years of wear. However, the best place for a Chinese carpet would be where its attractive design and colour can be seen to advantage and will complement the existing decor. They are ideally suited to a fairly formal living or dining room, or a bedroom.

NINGXIA IS A TOWN on the northern borders of China in the province of Ningxia and rug making in the area has been traced back to the Ming dynasty (1368–1644). The carpets produced in this area are the classic Chinese carpets. They usually have yellow or pink grounds with blue designs. Carpets were woven for Tibetan and Chinese Buddhist temples and monasteries throughout China and these, unlike their Islamic counterparts woven in Turkey and Persia, were designed with Buddhist, Taoist and general mystical and mythological motifs and symbols. Like Samarkand in Central Asia, Ningxia is positioned on an important trade route (in this case connecting China, Tibet and Mongolia). As a result, all the rugs sold in the town became known as Ningxia and the name became the generic term for a good-quality Chinese rug.

Peking rugs share certain characteristics with those made in Tientsin, the nearby port. They date from the Ch'ing dynasty (1644–c.1911) and are of good quality. Typically, Peking rugs feature symbolic motifs and medallions, such as the shou character, and also Buddhist, Taoist and Confucian motifs, as well as floral designs. Motifs are not normally joined by linking patterns (as would be the case in Islamic rugs), but they float independently on the background colour. The Peking workshops began to decline in the 1920s, when the American fashion for chinoiserie faded. Copies of Peking designs may be found in lower-quality Indian rugs and are also woven in Taiwan.

Tibetans have always travelled widely and adapted design elements from other cultures. The strongest influences have come from the south and east, e.g. Buddhist, Confucian and Taoist, but also from West Asia. Since the Dalai Lama fled to India in 1959, many Tibetan weavers have emigrated to Nepal, where they have set up carpet workshops.

△ A triple-peony design from Tibet with leaves on a beige ground and ocean, mountain and sky motifs surrounded by a border of vines and trellis.

◁ A Peking rug with a large central shou medallion and small shou and fu characters in the border. The shou and fu characters are symbols of longevity and happiness.

▷ This Tibetan carpet features a large, central lotus motif flanked by two phoenix and two dragons with stylized cloud motifs, all on a white ground.

◁ This 19th-century abstract black and gold rug, woven in Tibet, has a repeated Y motif in the centre. The borders feature a repeated geometric fret design alternating with the curved shapes of flowers.

△ A two-seat Ningxian temple rug, with a medallion of fo-dogs and realistic floral motifs on a bluish-red ground, with a border of individual flower motifs.

◁ A very fine 18th-century Ningxia dragon carpet in deep blue and gold, showing the five-clawed imperial dragon.

△ A traditional blue and white Peking rug. Its motifs seem to float in space and appear not to be joined to one another.

◁ A 19th-century Tibetan rug, with a wool and cotton pile in fret and cloudband design, using deep blue and white for a striking effect.

• Paotao

• Kansu

TIBET CHINA

NEPAL

CHARACTERISTICS

Colours are very different from Islamic carpets, being based on several basic tints including peach, apricot, blue, white, pinkish-red, black and brown with the use of shading to achieve a harmonious rug. Main colours are often yellow and blue, symbolic of earth and sky. In carpets woven before the second half of the 19th century, the ground is usually yellow and in later carpets it is often blue. The border, which is frequently filled with floral or geometric motifs, is often in contrast in both colour and style to the main field of the carpet.

WEAR

Most rugs have a woollen pile and all use the Senneh (asymmetrical) knot. They are made to a very high quality and will last a long time, even with a certain amount of wear.

HOME USE

Rugs that have been chemically washed to make them appear old are woven in traditional Chinese as well as Persian designs and, in many cases, it is difficult to distinguish between antique and contemporary. They may not be a sensible way of investing, but they are definitely an asset to the modern interior.

UNIVERSAL MOTIFS

IN CHINA, ARTISTIC symbols are common to all genres and techniques. Their meanings have remained unchanged over many centuries. Among the most common is the fo-dog, which represents protection from evil; the dragon, the union of earthly and celestial forces; the lotus flower, purity and summer; the peony, respect and wealth; the stag and stork, longevity; the cloud, divine power; mountains and water, stability on a stormy sea; the bat, fortune; the swastika, cosmic rotation; and the ideograms shou and fu, fortune.

In the region of Kansu, carpets are lively and colourful, with decorations similar to those in Turkestan and widespread use of a layout consisting of three octagonal medallions in a row. The bulo motif is a tiny red, white and blue disc that is often spread across the field. Fields are blue with designs in bright red or orange. Paotao, the capital of Suiyuan province, is known for its large, colourful landscapes with animals. They are generally finely knotted, short pile in blues, greens, reds and yellows.

The border acts as a window onto the field of a rug. Unlike the border of an Islamic rug, it is not seen as a fundamental element that is there to complete the field, but as a separate frame for the important central design. Among the designs most commonly used in borders are fret motifs, often with three-dimensional effects, swastikas and floral motifs, particularly naturalistic peonies and lotus flowers. A characteristic decoration of minor borders is the so-called pearl motif, which is made up of small, white discs, usually on a blue ground.

▷ Many motifs are seen here: birds, butterflies, fish and lotus flowers within mountains, clouds and ocean borders.

△ These small medallions contain an abstract version of the chrysanthemum which is a popular Chinese motif. The wave motif, used as a frame, is often found in Chinese carpets.

△ Large medallions can be found on many Chinese carpets. This one is made up of small floral motifs, leaves and clouds. The individual floral sprays, floating separately on a dark field,

▷ The dragon is important to Chinese beliefs and designs. This one, clutching a pearl in each claw, symbolizes its function as guardian of the moon.

101

TIBET

Lhasa ●

NEPAL

CHARACTERISTICS

Rugs woven with tiger and leopard images, abstract stripes, full skin pelts, three-dimensional body and head designs, paw prints and spots (although only pelt rugs are officially classed as tiger rugs in the trade).

WEAR

Woven in Himalayan wool, these are good quality, hard-wearing carpets which will last for many decades, even when walked on in areas of heavy traffic.

HOME USE

Good welcoming rugs for a hall, or could be used in modern living rooms. Pictorial tigers should have a place, perhaps on a wall, where the complete picture can be viewed and enjoyed to the full.

TIGER RUGS

THE CAT RUGS OF Paotao were woven in the early 20th century. Paotao is close to Mongolia, a cold, rugged and dusty land, and the rugs were used for sitting or sleeping on. But tigers and leopards have been portrayed in Tibetan rugs for over 100 years. They were originally woven for the high lama to sit on, but as the animals became scarcer, rugs woven with tiger and leopard images, abstract stripes, full skin, three-dimensional body and head designs, paw prints and spots appeared.

The term "tiger rug" usually refers to rugs woven in Tibet, although such carpets are woven in the same regions as carpets with dragon designs too. The designs are usually based on tiger skins rather than on the live animal, but occasionally it may be highly abstract with perhaps a small square of stripes surrounded by a wide border. Some rugs provide realistic, almost cartoon-like representations of tigers, but they are not always classed as tiger rugs in the trade. Tigers are the lords of the mountains and woods, joint controllers of winds and water, the traditional enemy of the dragon and associated with strength, virility and the West. Symbolically, stylized tiger rugs often represent aspects of Tantric meditation. Excellent copies of old tiger rugs are produced in large numbers today in Tibetan/Nepalese workshops.

△ A stylized flayed tiger skin in navy blue on a buff ground, woven in Tibet during the second half of the 20th century.

◁ This leopard pelt rug was woven by Tibetans now working in Nepal. It is very life-like and was probably copied from an earlier version.

▽ Tiger stripes are framed by a series of light-to-dark colours in this "window" carpet, giving it an abstract quality typical of modern pieces.

△ A leaping tiger, woven in China c. 1920, with mountains, clouds and sea and surrounded by a border of fret motifs.

◁ A large, lifelike tiger gazing irately at a small bird on the branch of a tree. Unusually, no border is used on this 1920s Chinese rug.

EUROPE

Spain is the only European nation that has an ancient tradition of carpet making. Due to the centuries of Arab domination, carpets have been woven there ever since the 12th century. During the 17th century, weavers in many European countries were inspired by the Persian masterpieces from Isfahan, Kashan and Tabriz – and also by Turkish pieces – to make their own carpets. Each country took on the Eastern compositions and adapted them to their own decorative traditions, producing items that were unique to each country.

The establishment of distinctive European styles was spearheaded by the French Savonnerie workshops and, in fact, the term Savonnerie is often applied generically to all hand-knotted carpets of European origin. Specifically, however, it relates to those carpets that were made by the French national carpet manufactory established in 1627 at Chaillot (in a former soap factory). It was transferred from there in 1826 to the Gobelins in Paris (the Royal

In the 17th century, European carpet making was largely inspired by carpets imported from Persia and Turkey, whose designs were developed and adapted. Later in the century, distinctive European styles emerged.

Tapestry Workshop founded by Louis XIV in 1667), where the work still continues today. The Savonnerie technique produces very closely woven, deeply luxurious piled wool carpets.

Several north European countries had a long tradition of peasant weaving, which has now sadly died out, but many European artists are rediscovering their old traditions, often based on past techniques and motifs, but appearing in a modern idiom. Scandinavia always produced characteristically flat-woven rugs and cushions, the best known being rölakans from Skåne, a southern province of Sweden. Rya rugs from Finland are coarsely woven loop-pile peasant rugs that were very popular in the 1960s and 1970s. Examples are often dated and initialled by the makers. Several of the Balkan countries have retained their own tradition of folk and peasant weaving in spite of – or possibly as an effect of – centuries of Ottoman rule and other influences.

ROMANIA & BESSARABIA

CHARACTERISTICS

Usually made by the slit-weave technique with all-over floral designs, often in bright "peasant" colours. Designs may be either geometric and stylized or quite realistic.

WEAR

Romanian and Bessarabian rugs are usually woven on cotton or wool warps. The pile wool is fairly good quality and the dyes come from Germany. Romanian rugs are given the names of towns, rivers and mountains, but this has nothing to do with where they are woven: the names are used to classify the quality of rugs in terms of knots per square foot. Such quality designations include (in order of merit, best first) cotton warp and weft: Milcov, Olt, Mures, Brailu, Bucharest; woollen warp and weft: Postavaro, Harmon, Brasov, Transylvania; mercerized cotton pile: Muldova.

HOME USE

The floral and folkloric styles of Romanian and Bessarabian rugs make them particularly suitable for homes with a Bohemian or eclectic style, and for bedrooms and possibly bathrooms. They can also be charming when thrown over the backs of armchairs and sofas.

ROMANIAN RUG WEAVING can be traced back to the days when the Balkan peninsula was controlled by the Ottoman empire from the 15th to the 19th centuries. But Romania, more than any of its neighbours, managed to retain its ethnic, cultural and religious identity. Romanian kilims combine their own fold-weaving traditions with those of Anatolian (Turkish) rug and kilim production.

Large numbers of rugs were exported to Europe via western Turkey during the 17th and 18th centuries and many of the rugs from that time still survive in churches in the Transylvanian region.

Romania's importance as a weaving centre is due not only to its past but also to the very effective organization of its many weavers. As in China, the central government established strict standards of quality in the rug industry and has exerted controls on both colour and design. Rugs are usually woven with the Persian (Senneh) knot on aluminium looms. The advantage of these looms over wooden is that they remain rigid, even in very humid atmospheres and the rugs are less likely to become misshapen. Most kilims woven in Romania today are made specifically for export, but more traditional items are produced as well. The technique used is predominantly slit-weave, in a range of designs taken mainly from Turkish, Caucasian and sometimes Persian designs, often in somewhat paler colours. Romania has been the most successful Balkan weaving country of the 20th century. Sadly, political problems have destabilized production and export, at least for the time being.

Bessarabia is a close neighbour to Romania. Situated in south-west Ukraine, it produces flat-woven kilims. These often show the influence of Turkish weaving and generally have repeat floral sprays on a predominantly black or beige ground. Although quite a number of these rugs are still available, their prices can be high because they have become increasingly popular during the 1980s and 1990s, particulary 18th- and 19th-century examples.

△△ A rare and valuable Bessarabian flat-weave carpet from the Ukraine, woven *c.* 1870, with curvilinear floral sprays on a deep blue ground.

△ This Romanian kilim features delicately drawn, realistic floral motifs in pretty pale colours. The design is framed with a simple olive green surround.

△ A 19th-century
Romanian kilim with an
extremely elaborate design
of flower sprays, tendrils
and leaves. The interest is
all in the main design —
there is no border.

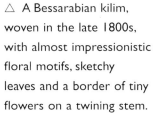

△ A Bessarabian kilim,
woven in the late 1800s,
with almost impressionistic
floral motifs, sketchy
leaves and a border of tiny
flowers on a twining stem.

▷ An Bessarabian
kilim, woven in the
late 19th century, in a
riotous profusion of
garden flowers on a
very deep ground.

△ A floral kilim with rows of medallions, each
filled with a flower motif and bordered with
curling leaves that are all highly curvilinear.

SCANDINAVIA

SCANDINAVIA HAS A long tradition of weaving natural homespun, flat-weave and shaggy, colourful rugs that are necessary in order to cope with the long, dark days of the Scandinavian winter. This is a home or cottage industry with a continuous tradition over the centuries. It has never died out but has evolved, particularly during the 20th century, to produce highly modern designs and patterns that are based on ancient motifs.

Rya rugs are double-pile rugs, thick and shaggy, made for warmth in various parts of Scandinavia (especially Finland) and they may have been inspired by the animal skins that would originally have been used as rugs and coverlets. They date back at least to the 10th century and were used both as floor coverings and bed covers. They were initially in plain colours but, by the late 18th century, they were being decorated with designs taken from pattern books imported from France and Germany.

The double-weave Scandinavian rugs and cushions from the south of Sweden, known as rölakans, also have a particular boldness in juxtapositions of clear, bright colours together with that clarity and simplicity of design that is peculiar to Scandinavia. They were often woven in wide stripes or repeating interlocking triangles using plain- rather than slit-weave technique. These rugs use patterns that seem to have survived, more or less unchanged, since Viking times.

CHARACTERISTICS

Geometric, often abstract designs of great style and boldness, in a variety of confident colours varying from browns and blacks or juxtapositions of blues and greens, to primary colours or black and white. Rugs may have a long, shaggy pile (as in rya rugs) or plain-weave (rölakan).

WEAR

Scandinavian rugs are nearly always made of wool and produced with care for their durable properties, so they are extremely hard-wearing. Rya rugs, in particular, should be shaken frequently, but vacuumed with care so that the long yarns of the pile do not get pulled.

HOME USE

These rugs, with their positive, clearly delineated patterns, bold colours and warm and rough textures, are ideal as foils for the modern minimalist interior. They go equally well with pale woods as with metal and glass furniture, adding contrast to what might otherwise be a rather cold environment.

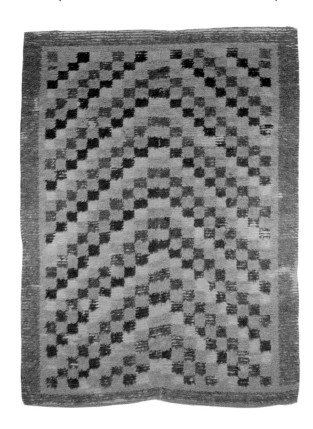

△ This 18th-century Finnish rug has a typical design of checked stripes in natural colours.

△ A Finnish rug, woven in 1822, featuring a pictorial design of stylized flowers and figures.

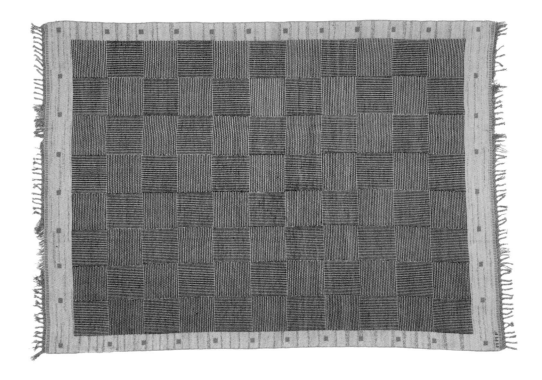

△ This rug was woven around 1923 in Sweden. The overall grey is lifted by the way in which the light catches the woven squares and the small red squares in the border.

△ The design of this Swedish rug shows some influence from oriental carpets, particularly in the tree-of-life pattern, which is repeated throughout.

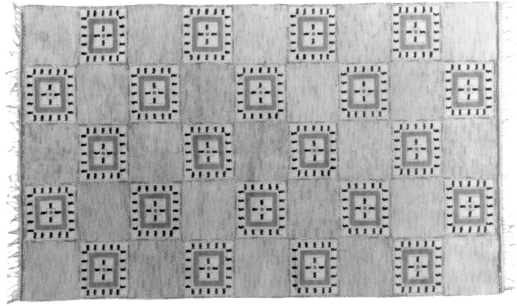

▷ This Swedish rug is simple, subtle and yet as arresting as one comes to expect from the best of Scandinavian design.

FRANCE

• Paris

• Aubusson

CHARACTERISTICS

Curvilinear, floral designs with large cabbage roses, usually based on a central medallion with intertwining floral motifs within it and round the borders. Savonnerie carpets have a velvety pile; Aubussons may be either flat- or pile-weave.

WEAR

Both types of carpet are hard-wearing, with Savonnerie carpets being the equivalent of oriental knotted-pile carpets and Aubussons being the equivalent of flat-weave kilims.

HOME USE

The style of these carpets just asks for a place where they can be admired and appreciated, so they look at their finest in uncluttered rooms with a traditional flavour. They probably appear best in well-proportioned rooms with high ceilings and "important"-looking furniture.

FRANCE

SEVENTEENTH-CENTURY French hand-knotted carpets are rare today, but examples from the Savonnerie and Aubusson workshops are much sought after. The name Savonnerie is a term that is often applied generically to all hand-knotted carpets of French origin and indicates pile carpets of extreme luxury. The Savonnerie workshop was founded in 1627 in Chaillot in a former soap works. From the start, the intention was to produce carpets of superb technical quality using only the best materials and the finest knotting with a deep, velvet-like pile. Carpets were woven purely for the court or the state and closely reflected the tastes of the period: heavy, scrolling acanthus leaves and dark grounds during Louis XIV's reign; rococo with twisting leaves and floral swags during the time of Louis XV; and a more restrained style for Louis XVI.

At Aubusson, an early tapestry-weaving centre, two completely different types of carpet were woven: pile carpets similar, but inferior to those from the Savonnerie, in weaving and materials, and flat-woven carpets using the tapestry technique, which were quicker, easier and cheaper, and were bought by the nobility and better-off merchants. They followed the stylistic evolution of Savonnerie carpets but had simpler designs. The style of both Savonnerie and Aubusson carpets had an enormous influence on overseas production so that between the end of the 18th century and the mid-19th century, the French carpet became – even in the Orient and especially in Anatolia – the model to imitate.

During the 19th century, a number of needlework schools came into existence in France and the United States, and a great many fine carpets were produced.

◁ This is a flat-weave Aubusson, woven in 1870 and typical of the style, with its subdued colours and the use of lush garden plants and curvilinear lines.

◁ This 19th-century Aubusson is rich in colour and intricate in design, though in a lighter vein than some, with separate elements and a very narrow outer border.

△ A light-hearted Aubusson incorporating summer flowers in swags and bouquets, the centre group in an oval border. The pale colour is fit for a lady's boudoir.

▷ Most Aubusson carpets were flat-woven, but a number of them (using very similar designs) were hand-knotted, like this rare example from the time of Charles X, c. 1825.

▽ This unusual needlepoint was made in France around 1850 and has a grid pattern of cultivated flowers within a floral and wavy border.

◁ This jazzy design was woven at Aubusson around 1930. Its pale central panel and rusty reds reflect the Aubusson tradition as well as a distinctive Art Deco look.

▽ This needlepoint-embroidered carpet is meticulously worked in stripes of alternating chevrons and floral bouquets, with a border of separated bouquets.

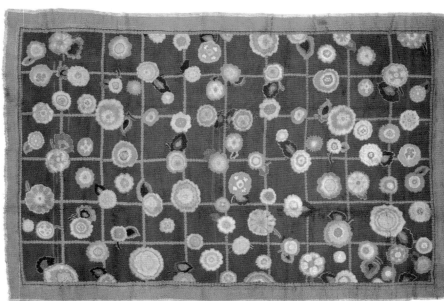

△ A whimsical and spirited Savonnerie carpet with stylized flowers on a rich mocha ground.

◁ A very fine Savonnerie carpet, woven *c.* 1930. It is reminiscent of an Italianate marble floor.

◁ A soft and luxurious Savonnerie carpet in pinks, red, gold and grey, with two medallions in the centre and a wealth of floral detailing.

UNITED KINGDOM

ENGLAND WAS THE first European country to create a local tradition of carpet making that could vie with foreign imports. Many were direct copies of the carpets imported from Turkey in the 16th century. However, the manufacturing technique was different. Flax was used for the warp, rather than the wool used in Turkish carpets, and the knots were less tightly compacted. English armorial motifs were included in the designs of the borders, often with a brief inscription and/or the date. A few carpets were made with new designs and most have repeating patterns, often of dense floral sprays. They were used in a variety of ways – on stools, as cushion covers, to cover cupboards and tables – but not often on floors.

By 1750, the manufacture of pile carpets had died out. Instead, patterned flat-weaves and reversible double-weaves were made at Kidderminster, Wilton, Mortlake and Norwich, as well as Kilmarnock in Scotland. In 1730, French weavers were smuggled into the country to make loop-pile rugs on treadle looms at Wilton. Several workshops were established by European émigrés; one at Fulham, which by 1753 employed 100 men and many apprentices, was later sold and transferred to Exeter, but only three of the carpets woven there still exist. Thomas Moore opened a workshop at Chiswell Street, Moorfields in London, for which the well-known architect Robert Adam designed several carpets for specific interiors, where the designs mirrored the painted, moulded plaster motifs on the ceilings.

Thomas Whiting of Axminster had had the idea of making pile carpets for some time before he visited the Fulham factory and saw how it could be done. The first carpet was made in 1755. His work was continued by his son and grandson, their success being ensured by commissions to make the carpets for the Royal Pavilion in Brighton. At the beginning of the 19th century, English chinoiserie motifs were popular at Axminster.

CHARACTERISTICS
Fine-quality, wool pile carpets with armorial and floral decoration, occasionally with very English touches such as a central medallion containing a dog in a basket. Rather more restrained than French Aubusson and Savonnerie carpets.

WEAR
The knotted-pile technique is not indigenous to Europe and it is the labour-intensive nature and the high cost of labour in Europe that has prevented its widespread use. Carpets made in this way are therefore rare. These collectors' pieces are hard-wearing (as are all wool carpets with fine knotting), but expert advice should be sought prior to their cleaning and repair.

HOME USE
These expensive and collectible carpets are not really intended for home use, except as show pieces in an area of light traffic.

◁ The starburst design of this English carpet, woven during the first half of the 20th century in restrained colours of pale creams and reds, is slightly reminiscent of Art Deco style.

▽ A very fine and intricate needlepoint carpet, woven *c.* 1830. The design is embroidered onto canvas and the pattern worked in rusty reds with pale greens and mauves inside tiny medallions.

△ A sophisticated and ornate Axminster rug, woven *c.* 1760, with a large floral medallion, feathered fans in the corners and a fret design running along the border.

▷ An early English carpet, woven *c.* 1780 at Axminster. The design is purely European with realistic flowers, seashells along the border and a large, oval medallion.

SPAIN
Medinceli
Madrid
Cuenca
Arraiolos
Alcaraz
PORTUGAL

CHARACTERISTICS

Seventeenth century and later carpet designs are European and eclectic, but earlier examples were strongly influenced by the East and feature geometric designs and kufic inscriptions. Heraldic carpets are long and narrow, with armorial devices.

WEAR

Because the knotting is not very tight and the wool is not of the best quality, these carpets may not wear as well as their counterparts from the East – particularly those which are worked with a needle, rather than woven. However, all hand-knotted wool carpets should last for several generations.

HOME USE

Old carpets are collectible and should be given a place of honour and light traffic. New carpets can enhance any living room or bedroom, whether they are hung on the walls or placed on the floor.

SPAIN & PORTUGAL

KNOTTED PILE TECHNIQUES were already known in Europe in some localities by the Middle Ages. They were introduced to Spain and Portugal at an early date, doubtless by the Moors. Eleanor of Castile, when she married the future Edward I of England in 1255, brought with her, as part of her dowry, a number of carpets which she used to decorate her palace apartments in London and mention is made of "tapis sarassinois", captured from the Moors by the French King Louis IX in the 14th century.

Surviving examples of Spanish carpets of the 14th and later centuries derive their designs partly from Eastern rugs and partly from contemporary European embroidery and weaving. Patterns were geometric but verging on the curvilinear and fairly large, all-over motifs were arranged in rows. Borders, as in Persian and Turkish carpets, were part of the general design, rather than separate frames for the main design, as in China. Early Spanish carpets were characterized by the so-called Spanish knot, which was attached to alternating single warp threads, giving a marked diagonal emphasis to the pile and the pattern. The Ghiordes or Turkish knot was not introduced to Spain until the 17th century.

Few of the European countries that manufactured carpets in the 17th and 18th centuries rivalled the French or English manufacturers in quality. Spain and Portugal followed French styles very closely. A factory was set up in Madrid under royal patronage in the late 18th century, in which carpets were woven closely following Savonnerie and Aubusson patterns. The weave, however, was rather coarser than the French carpets and the wool was of poorer quality, so the designs are less finely worked. In compensation for this, colours are usually stronger, brighter and bolder than the French models, which makes the rugs more suited to the greater intensity of the sunlight in the south. This kind of carpet making is still carried on in Madrid today.

△ This 18th-century Portuguese embroidered carpet is from Arraiolos and was woven c. 1720. It has a central medallion, intricate floral motifs and pretty, pale colours.

◁ This 16th-century Spanish woollen pile carpet was made at Alcaraz and has the arms of the Dominican order at the corners.

▽ The Spanish town of Cuenca produced coarsely woven carpets as early as the 11th century. This one, woven in the 16th century, shows a bold, yet intricate floral design.

▷ This early Spanish armorial carpet features the arms of La Cerda of Medinaceli, with thistles and a powerful, branched plant in the border.

THE AMERICAS

North American rug making first began as a homecraft, with the practical object of providing what comfort was possible amidst the hardships of the Colonial period. Woven carpets were relatively unknown before Independence and floors were covered with painted sailcloth or even sand. Before 1775, rag rugs that were woven on hand looms were sometimes placed on top of doors as draught excluders. They had stout, linen warps and were made from scraps of clothes and other textiles that were cut into strips. The narrow lengths of cloth, dictated by the width of the loom, were sewn together to make sizeable carpets.

Hooked rugs are the best known North American rugs. This is an ancient technique that was brought over to America by settlers from European countries. Short lengths of coloured materials were pulled through a loose canvas to form the pile. This technique was developed into a characteristic American homecraft.

North America is the home of colourful rag and hooked rugs as well as the tribal rugs of the Navajo. In South America, even before the Incas, weavers in Peru were producing the finest weaving the world has ever known.

Most of the hooked rugs that are available today were made around the 1850s, though probably a few were made before 1700.

The Navajo, living in the northern part of Arizona and New Mexico, have a unique tradition of weaving, both in design and technique. What originally started out as blankets is now often woven into a heavier form as rugs. They only started to weave in the 18th century, using unravelled red wool from American military uniforms and producing unique blankets and rugs with a diamond pattern called eye-dazzlers (for obvious reasons). In Central America, Mexico is well known for its rugs and blankets in flamboyant and flame-like colours.

Rugs and wall hangings are made throughout South America, in Peru, Bolivia, Colombia, Brazil, Argentina and Venezuela. Weavers in Peru have one of the longest weaving traditions in the world, using the silky soft wool of llamas to produce wonderfully fine rugs.

RAG & HOOKED RUGS

CHARACTERISTICS

Rag rugs were homely rugs that were made from a "rag bag" of cast-off and worn clothes and household textiles, and dyed to soft colours with local dyestuffs. Patchwork rugs were cut in "tongue" shapes and the pieces overlapped; braid and knitted rugs used the same materials, cut into strips and sewn or knitted together. All created practical, washable, durable floor finishes, without wasting materials. Where these techniques are used today, they use new materials; design and colour are important elements of the finished product, which is as much a work of art as a utility rug.

WEAR

Original rag rugs were backed and lined, and made for durability. Today's rugs (usually made with wool) are often made for show rather than for use, but the techniques produce hard-wearing pieces and, if washable fabrics are used, they should also be durable objects.

HOME USE

Sturdy, good-looking rugs which can be used in many different ways in various parts of the home. Modern examples can be designed specifically to fit in with a particular scheme.

IN NORTH AMERICA, the early colonials found it difficult to get materials and comforts for the home and many could not afford them. Hooked rugs, to soften and warm the floors, were made with materials from worn-out garments and other household textiles, which were coloured with local natural dyestuffs such as powdered bricks for pink, goldenrod for yellow, as well as onion skins, blueberries and hickory bark. The designs were naturalistic and not stylized, and marine designs were sometimes created by sailors or their wives.

French settlers in Quebec and Nova Scotia specialized in elaborate floral designs. Animal designs were also popular, with mottoes often included. The cottage industries of New England produced small amounts of the different types of basic, flat-woven carpets known variously as English, Scottish, Kidderminster, Kilmarnock, ingrain, Venetian, spotted or mottled. A rare example of a knotted-pile carpet, made by William Peter Sprague of Philadelphia in 1791, can be seen in the Smithsonian Institute in Washington. This carpet is basically an armorial design but apart from the central

eagle and devices of the States, it takes its motifs from French Aubussons. Sprague used to advertise as making Axminster, ingrain or carpets "in the Turkey manner". Edward Sands Frost, an invalided soldier, sold patterns made from metal stencils to the women of New England and built up a business that contintued to flourish up until the early 20th century.

The precursors of these floor rugs were the American bed rugs, using similar techniques of manufacture, which seem to have been used by a great many colonialists in the 17th century as a guard against the cold. In 1630, Governor John Winthrop wrote from Massachusetts to his son in England, "to bring a store of Coarse Rugges, bothe to use and to sell". The word rug may be directly descended from the Swedish "rugge"; and in Finland rugs were used as bedcovers. North American rugs were made with whatever materials were to hand and some are knotted, like the rag floor rugs of the late 19th century. Most were created with a hand-spun wool and were coarse and nubby, somewhat like the hooked rug that was to follow more than 100 years later.

◁ By the end of the 19th century, hooked rugs were made throughout North America. The central medallion of this example is filled by a delightful lion motif in natural beiges and browns.

◁ This woollen hooked rug features curling, naturalistic flowers framed by a flowing trellis border. The colours are fresh, pretty and pale, perfect for a feminine bedroom.

▷ This is a beautiful example of a modern hooked rug. The design is simplistically drawn, adding to its rustic appeal, and has the effect of a framed painting. Flowers, fruits and vegetables in rich, natural colours are traditional motifs in pictorial hooked rugs.

NAVAJO RUGS

NAVAJO RUGS HAVE a tremendous visual impact, which reflects the strength of Navajo culture and their tradition as a people. Weaving designs evolved from simple beginnings in the 18th century and became more elaborate in response to changing demands during the second half of the 19th century. Today, they have returned to a new-found simplicity. The actual method of weaving has remained virtually unchanged and is basically the tapestry- or flat-weave technique used in Middle Eastern kilims.

The Spanish introduced sheep into Old Navajo Land near New Mexico in the 16th century and the nomadic Navajo acquired large flocks from them and became famous for the blankets that they wove for their own use. During the complex history of banishment and then their return to a diminished territory, Navajo's weaving was influenced by many factors, including the shortage of wool and the weaving of their neighbours, the Pueblo Indians. When the Navajo first acquired their flocks, they spun the yarn from their own fleece and they have returned to this today. During the intervening period, they bought commercial yarns which were available in a range of strong, bright colours. Today's pieces are brightly coloured, sturdy and largely made up of stripes or diamond motifs. Unlike Middle Eastern work, individual Navajo weavers may become well-known for the quality of their weaving and designs, and a particular weaver's work can be more expensive than that of other weavers. The weaving is done by women who learn through a "watch and do" process.

CHARACTERISTICS

Designs are usually abstract and geometric, with long, vertical colour changes, but many are also pictorial, depicting objects of everyday life on a plain background. There may be images of a helicopter or a train, of trucks, or even of cartoon characters. Navajo rugs are worked in bright colours with a predominance of red.

WEAR

Similar to kilims in construction; woven in the same tapestry technique, producing a firm, durable, yet fairly flexible result. Various forms of dovetailing are used to prevent the changes in colour from leaving slits in the rug. Navajo weavers braid each edge as they weave to strengthen the selvedge. All four braids are tied together at the corners when the rug is taken off the loom, producing characteristic tassels.

HOME USE

These exuberant and lovely bright weavings can liven up any room, from a young person's encompass-all room to an informal living room. They look marvellous when thrown over a sofa and will act as a focus for attention if hung on a wall.

◁ An exceptional chief's blanket, woven during the latter part of the classic period of Navajo weaving (1850–1875). Worn about the shoulders, these were highly prized items, made primarily for export to neighbouring tribes such as the Cheyenne and Sioux.

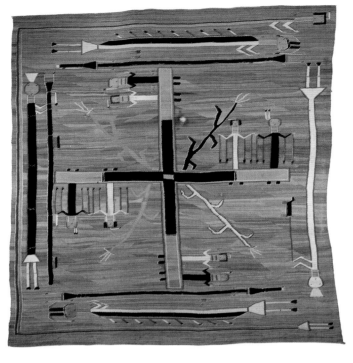

◁ Sand-painting rugs depict ceremonial paintings made of coloured sands, minerals and organic matter created by Navajo medicine men for healing purposes. This beautiful example features a "Whirling Log" painting on a field of variegated brown.

△ This rug has stepped and serrated geometric devices against a dark red field. Originally, the Navajo bought red baize from local Spaniards and unravelled it strand by strand to use in their rugs.

◁ This four-in-one sampler rug features stepped and sawtoothed geometric devices on a vibrant multi-coloured field. The pictorial design elements include hogans, bows, buckets, boots, arrows and hats.

SOUTH AMERICA

PERUVIAN WEAVING HAS one of the longest histories in the world. The valleys of Chancay in the central coastal region have produced a great variety of sophisticated items and Chancay culture (100 BC–AD 1200) cultivated cotton for dyed patterned cloth. Peoples in the high altitudes of Arica, Paracas and Mazca cultures used wool from llamas and vicunas. The Incas (1430–1532) inherited 3,000 years of weaving skills and traditions, weaving the finest textiles for burning as ritual offerings. South America has a wide variety of raw materials and techniques with which they make clothing, woven furnishings and decorative items. Fibre from trees, plants and shrubs, bird feathers, linen and cotton were all used in the pre-Columbian period and llama, alpaca and vicuna were used some 3,000 years ago. Pre-Columbian weavers produced a great variety of fabrics including flat-weaves.

Today, textiles still play an important role in everyday life. Each region has its own individual yarns, methods of weaving and designs. For example, in the Aymara cultures of the islands of Lake Titicaca, each family owns four different types of colourful costume: for work, leisure, weddings and festivals. In Peru, Bolivia, Ecuador and Colombia, both women and men have particular costumes. Andean peoples still use principally camelid wools, which can be spun into fine, shiny yarn that has a texture not unlike silk. Rugs, wall hangings and other items of woven furnishings are now made in several centres including Tintorero in Venezuela, La Guajira and San Jacinto in Colombia, Otarolo in Salasaca, Ayacucho and San Pedro de Cajas in Peru, Villa Ribera in Bolivia, Santa Maria de Catamarca in Argentina and Timbauba in the north of Brazil. Almost all are designed for sale to Europe or North America.

CHARACTERISTICS

Rugs and hangings throughout South America vary enormously, from fine, firm yarns in dark colours with brilliant red strips to loosely woven, very soft, silky yarns in vegetable-dyed pastel pinks, browns, blues and greys. Designs may be geometric and abstract or pictorial.

WEAR

Most of the weavings are not really suitable for use on the floor. They are either too fine and will ruck and slip, or too soft and will not wear well.

HOME USE

These weavings are delightful and have a particularly indigenous quality, in both abstract and figurative form. They can be used on walls in any room in the home – children, in particular, will enjoy the strange birds and scenery of the pictorial weavings.

△ A striking contemporary rug made from undyed wool in Ayacucho, Peru. It features traditional pre-Columbian designs in natural browns and beiges.

△ Alternating rows of pink and grey serrated motifs produce a slight optical illusion effect in this rug. The wool was dyed using natural materials.

△ This wall hanging was woven in San Pedro de Cajas, Peru, using unspun wool. The colourful design depicts an idealized picture of rural village life complete with marketplace and bell tower.

▷ The rows of stylized animals on this delightful contemporary rug are arranged on diagonal stripes so that they seem to be climbing up a hill.

CONTEMPORARY DESIGNS

After the decline of European hand-knotted carpet making in the late 17th century, there was a revival of English rug making in the second half of the 18th century, when some excellent carpets were produced. Hand-knotted carpets continue to be made in small quantities all over Europe, and usually for the luxury market. William Morris produced a series of carpets with his hallmark of simple designs, based on Persian classical designs. During the 1920s, the Bauhaus in Germany produced several meticulously designed and characteristically unconventional carpets, yet with a strong sense of discipline and nearly all of these are now in private collections.

During the 1930s, France, with its sense of proportion, colour, luxury and frivolity, ensured that it

Many new carpet designs have emerged during the 20th century, from Arts & Crafts, through Art Nouveau, Art Deco and Modernist. Rug design today is mostly abstract and takes its inspiration from a myriad sources.

had a clear leadership in Art Deco designs and some of the best rugs came from French designers. Jean-François Thomas, René Herbst and Maurice Dufrène all designed painterly rugs. Dufrène was one of the best known French designers, who made the transition from Art Nouveau and worked right through the whole of the Art Deco period and into the 1940s.

From 1930, a group of English artists and architects created a sequence of hand-tufted wool rugs commissioned for limited production by the Wilton Royal Carpet Manufacturing Company. They included John Tandy, Ronald Grierson and Marian Dorn. Marian Dorn in particular ("the mistress of the modernist rug") has left her mark by the rugs she designed specifically for white-painted and uncluttered, modern homes.

CHARACTERISTICS

Simple, Gothic designs based on nature, i.e. flowers and foliage, with a tendency to deep, rich blues, greens and reds. Generally following the Islamic patterns but with a definite simplicity and Gothic feeling.

WEAR

Well-made rugs; many are still in the homes and colleges for which they were designed and woven. Very collectible and although eminently durable, these are not intended for hard wear. Any carpet manufactured by Morris is now extremely expensive, as are the Donegal carpets designed by Voysey.

HOME USE

Morris rugs are very expensive. Any rug in the same style would go well in a simple, unaffected interior with wooden furniture and panelling.

ARTS & CRAFTS

IN 1801, THE JACQUARD loom was introduced to the world and from then on, it was possible to weave intricate designs by machine. By 1820, the loom was in use for carpets in Philadelphia and, by 1838, there were over 2,000 looms in Kidderminster. It immediately became fashionable to buy machine-made carpets for the home because they were durable and cheap. The Arts & Crafts movement originated in Britain where, for more than 50 years before the formation of the Arts & Crafts Exhibition Society in 1888, designers, architects and theorists had deplored the aesthetic and social effects of industrialization. The American architect Frank Lloyd Wright thought the machine could be used to fulfil the Arts & Crafts vision of design and the style was taken up by furniture manufacturers, and carpets were woven to similar designs by established carpet manufacturers such as Bigelow & Co.

The British exponents of the Arts & Crafts movement wanted to return to traditional values of craftsmanship and to provide a work ethic that went back to Gothic architecture and tied in with Christian morality. John Ruskin and William Morris are the names most associated with Arts & Crafts in England, but many others were involved, including A. W. Pugin, Charles Rennie Mackintosh, Walter Crane and C. F. A. Voysey, all of whom produced designs for carpets.

William Morris is probably the best-known carpet designer of the 19th century and he designed carpets for commercial companies before producing hand-knotted pieces at his Hammersmith workshop, which were always known as "Hammersmith carpets", even after the workshop moved to Merton Abbey. A visitor to the carpet workshop at Merton wrote:

"It is not crowded. In the middle sits a woman finishing off some completed rugs; in a corner is a large pile of worsted of a magnificent red, heaped becomingly into a deep-coloured straw basket. One of the rugs being made is of silk instead of worsted, very exquisite in quality and surface. It is a delightful workroom."

▷ This rare Arts & Crafts carpet was woven in Donegal, Ireland, c. 1905. The positive, rich colours were popular at the time.

△ Although oriental designs have obviously influenced this Arts & Crafts carpet, its simplified form and colours are more typical of European carpets.

△ This Donegal carpet has a very curvilinear and intricate design in the somewhat pale and subtle colours popular in Europe.

▷ Distinctive Art Nouveau tendencies can be seen in this Arts & Crafts carpet, in the stylized roses and the elongated, sinuous foliage that forms the trellis.

◁ A pale and interesting carpet, rare in both colour and design. It was woven in Donegal at the turn of the 20th century.

129

ART DECO

ART DECO IS THE name for the decorative arts of the 1920s and 1930s in Europe and America, and it sprang from the Paris Exposition Internationale des Arts Decoratifs et Industriels Modernes in 1925. Characteristic of Art Deco was the vogue for a streamlined style, with inspiration from archaeological finds in Egypt, Diaghilev's Ballet Russe, cubism, Mayan and Aztec cultures, and what it contributed to carpet style was the idea of carpet designs being created by well-known artists, designers and architects. The 1920s, in particular, saw an upsurge in popularity of "designer" carpets. Morris & Co paved the way for an increased interest in European textiles generally, although the number of designers making rugs in the modern style remained small, compared with those providing modern designs in other media. The role of the rug was no longer simply as a decorative floor finish, but an integral part of the whole scheme.

During the 1920s, many rugs were woven in Belgium and they often had abstract patterns or motifs in sombre colours. Some designers worked with machine-weaving companies and in England, Axminster, Wilton Royal, Edinburgh Weavers and Templeton set up specialist departments for weaving designer rugs that they commissioned from well-known designers such as Eileen Gray, Frank Brangwyn, Marian Dorn and her husband, and the American-born Edward McKnight Kauffer. Chinese-born Betty Joel wove to commission and had her rugs made in China. In France, many rugs were commissioned for exhibitions and luxury liners.

Designers and studios involved included Jacques-Emile Ruhlmann, Paul Follot and the firm of Süe et Marie. In northern Africa, the Myrbor Studio wove designs by Jean Lurçat, Fernand Lèger, Joan Miró and Jean Arp, among others. In the USA, Ruth Reeves designed rugs evoking American city life, as well as cubist and geometrical motifs, while Donald Deskey, Gilbert Rohde, Eugene Schoen and Loma Saarinen all designed rugs for Cranbrooke Academy.

▷ This is a rare example of an Art Deco/Modernist carpet, designed by Betty Joel c. 1930 and including her monogram (in the bottom right corner of the picture).

▷ An Art Deco/Modernist carpet designed by Edward McKnight Kauffer, woven by Royal Wilton, c. 1930.

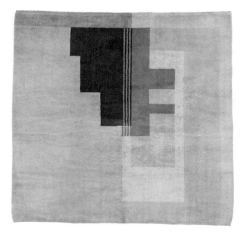

▽ This charming and rare Art Deco/Modernist carpet was woven by Royal Wilton, c. 1937. It was obviously specially designed for a music room.

△ A French Art Deco carpet, c. 1925, with a very bold design possibly symbolizing some form of industrial machine.

◁ This Art Deco carpet, c. 1935, has the popular pale colour called porridge, with minimal decoration in blues and greens with a touch of red.

THE NEW DESIGNERS

TODAY, ARTISTS AND designers cooperate with weavers in all carpet-making countries, both in the Orient and in the West. Variations of traditional or modern designs are woven in villages and workshops of weaving communities, specifically for sale to the West. The quality of the weaving is excellent, as are the yarns and dyes used. Both Turkey and India have produced rugs and carpets to new designs sent out to them from Europe or America. The designs are often abstract and make interesting use of colour combinations and tonalities. Weaving groups, who have for centuries woven their own traditional designs and motifs, have shown a capacity for understanding and interpreting these designs with great versatility. Designs may be woven as limited editions, as one-offs or as multiple production. The quality of technique and interpretation of designs and of the dyeing is normally excellent.

One interesting development is the advent of the modern artist/weaver. Artist/weavers have often trained first as artists or designers and then taken to weaving their own designs on their own looms. These pieces are often flat-woven using the tapestry technique and usually have the quality of modern works of art. Their designs are likely to be abstract, with an emphasis on line and colour. This is a form of carpet making that has never died out in Scandinavia, where the peasant weaving tradition has evolved into increasingly sophisticated modern designs during the 20th century and has also influenced design in other countries. The Danish textile artists Jette Kastberg and Jette Kai, for example, weave woollen flat-weave carpets, interpreting the traditional geometric Scandinavian patterns found on old embroidered or woven cloth and incorporating these elements into their work.

CHARACTERISTICS

The carpet is viewed as a work of art – designs will often be geometric, colourful and individual. Alternatively, they may be very subtle. Modern artist-designed carpets may be hand-knotted, plain-weave or even woven by machine.

WEAR

Almost all artist-designed rugs are well-made and of good-quality materials, since they are often woven to commission and expensive. Modern machine carpet-making techniques mean that it is possible to commission a design for a rug, or for a border on a rug, or to ring the changes in colour and pattern. These are usually best-quality carpets and they will withstand the hardest of use.

HOME USE

Most of these rugs are, like traditional oriental carpets, one-offs. They may be found at exhibitions or in specialist shops, where they can be chosen to fit in with a decor that exists. Alternatively, they can be commissioned, in which case the client can discuss colour and pattern preferences and other requirements with the artist, and get something truly individual and personal.

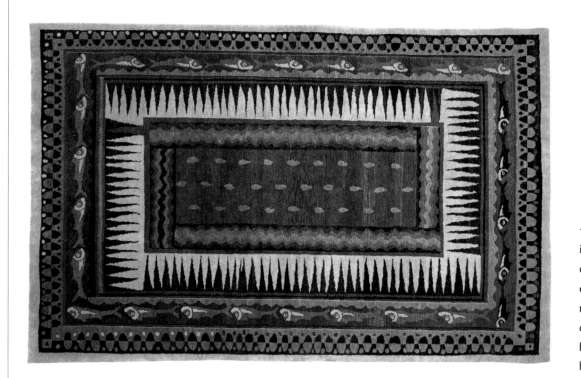

◁ This rug, woven in Turkey to a contemporary design, would look marvellous as a centrepiece, either laid on the floor or hung on a wall.

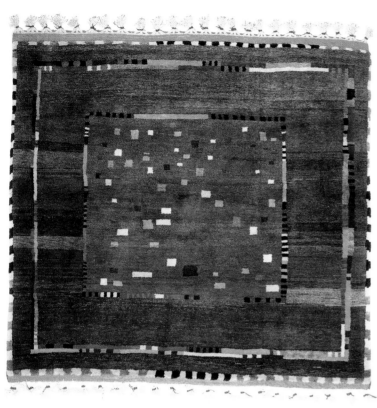

◁ A modern "window" rug, woven in a Turkish village. The warp ends have been tied into short fringes.

▷ Two runners that have been woven in Turkey, showing interesting variations on what might be a tiger stripe theme.

△ Contemporary design woven in Himalayan wool treated with Swiss dyes by Tibetan weavers working in Nepal.

▷ The traditional motif in the centre of this rug was woven and designed by rural village weavers in Turkey, but has a definitely modern, abstract look.

▷ Entitled "Diamond Dust Shoes" and designed by Andy Warhol, this is an example of the rug as a conscious work of art.

▷ A simple, borderless raindrop design in rich reds and yellows. This rug would be a good choice for a hall.

▽ Bold designs, such as this tan, cream and black rug, would look splendid in a modern setting.

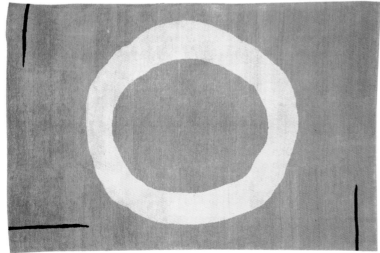

▷ The lovely castellated design of this carpet, with its colourful abstract shapes, could grace a traditional hearth just as well as a modern room.

▽ This beautiful, bold design, with its shapely lines, has a similar quality to many traditional animal pelt rugs.

▷ This rug design, entitled "Lettres Imperiales" and based on a collage, is consciously a work of art.

◁ A very subtle rug designed in England and woven in Turkey. Such pale colours particularly suit modern interior styles.

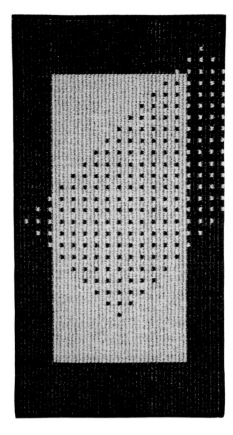

△ A marvellous freeform scribble marks this charming, informal, flat-woven rug.

◁ A deceptively simple two-tone flat-weave, designed and woven in England. This rug would visually lift, say, a hall, living room or dining room or hang from the wall.

△ The versatile, deceptively simple design of this rug, could equally make a bold statement in a modern interior or blend into the background of a more eclectic home.

▷ This rich and subtle rug which could adorn any room in the home was designed and woven in England.

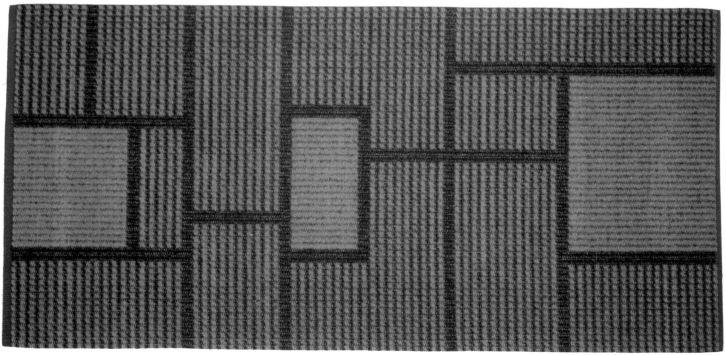

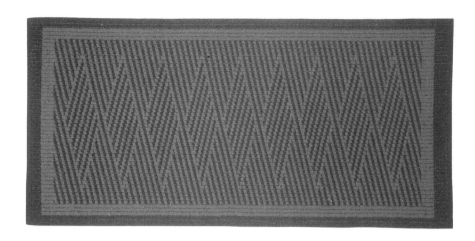

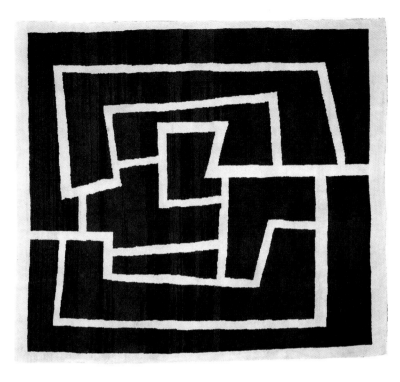

△ A bold and attractive "diaper" diamond pattern flat-woven rug, created with stripes on a blue ground.

△▷ The bold, angular design in black and white would provide a warm complement to modern, sleek, hard surfaces and minimal colour schemes.

▷ This pretty soft, red kilim with subtle stripes, makes good use of abrash colour variations.

◁ Stripes within stripes in rich blue and red create a simple and fun design, a rug to "cheer the cockles" of any room.

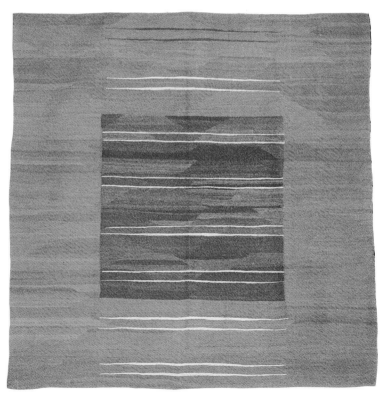

PRACTICAL
POINTERS

Carpet-making Techniques

A knowledge of the techniques and materials used to make rugs and carpets will help you both to recognize a particular type and to understand its intrinsic qualities. In this way, you will be able to make an informed decision when choosing a carpet for your home. For example, the type of knot used to make a pile carpet will not only affect its design but also its durability, so it is well worth being aware of such factors before making a purchase.

HAND-KNOTTED PILE CARPETS

A pile carpet is made by hand-knotting rows of dyed woollen yarns onto warp threads that are already stretched onto the loom. The hand-knotted yarns form the pile of the carpet. After each row of knots, one or two rows of weft threads are woven in and beaten down to give a tightly compacted, firm carpet. Continuous rows of knots and weft are worked like this across the width of the loom. When the entire carpet has been knotted, the ends of the warp strands are cut away from the loom and the carpet is then taken down. The pile is clipped to the required height by specialized workers using flat shears and the carpet is then washed in running water to soften it and dried in the sun to set the colours and to bleach slightly any that are too bright.

Tribal weavers may keep the patterns of their carpets in their heads, often remembering a large number of small patterns and using them in a variety of combinations and colours. Tribal weavings, therefore, tend to be made up of fairly small sized motifs that are often repeated. Workshop weavers, both in cities and villages, tend to use a "cartoon" of the carpet design, drawn in graph form, as a template.

Two different types of knots are used in the Middle East: the Persian (or Senneh) asymmetrical knot and the Turkish (or Ghiordes) symmetrical knot. Turkish knots give a slightly more full-bodied consistency to the carpet, but both of these knots are equally durable. In spite of their names, both knots are used everywhere (the Ghiordes knot is even used in Senneh). In general, the symmetrical knot is more suitable for geometrical designs and the asymmetrical knot, which is smaller and irregular, is better for curvilinear motifs. Each knot involves two strands of the warp at a time. In the Ghiordes knot, the yarn is wrapped around both warp strands and then the two ends are looped around the warp strands and drawn back out to protrude between the strands. The two free ends form the tuft of the pile. In the Senneh knot, the yarn is wound round one warp strand and looped under and drawn back round the

BASIC DOUBLE-WARP KNOTS

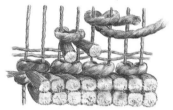

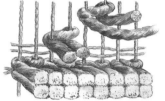

△ Symmetrical Turkish (Ghiordes) knot in which the wool is wrapped around two adjacent warps. Generally used for geometric designs.

△ Asymmetrical Persian (Senneh) knot in which the wool is also wrapped around two adjacent warps. Generally used for curvilinear designs.

FALSE (JUFTI) AND SINGLE-WARP KNOTS

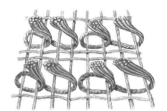

△ The symmetrical false knot takes in four warp threads and is therefore faster to weave though less dense than the double-warp knots.

△ Asymmetrical false knot, which also takes in four warp threads. It is generally used for curvilinear rather than geometric designs.

△ The Spanish knot is unknown in the Orient. The wool is wrapped around a single warp only and alternating warps are left unknotted.

other, leaving the two ends of the tuft separated by the one free strand. You can see the difference between the symmetrical and asymmetrical systems just by folding the pile horizontally in the direction of the weft and examining a row of knots.

The jufti (or false) knot is a variation in which the pile yarn is wrapped round four warp strands, rather than two. This ancient knot was originally created to achieve particular effects, but in recent times it has been used to increase the speed of weaving, although it produces inferior carpets. There are both symmetrical and asymmetrical versions of the false knot. Another ancient knot, hardly ever used in the Orient but used in

▷ These Indian women are completing the final stage in the process of making a pile carpet. They are clipping the pile with small sheers to produce an even finish.

Spain since the 12th century, is the Spanish (or single-warp) knot, in which the pile yarn is wrapped round a single thread of the warp, alternating even and odd threads and leaving the two free ends of the knot at the sides of the warp.

Technical aspects of weaving, particularly the number of knots within a given measure (usually 4in/10cm square) are considered to be the essential aspects of a rug's quality. The quality of a carpet is not to do with the thickness of the pile, but the closeness of the weave and both thick and thin yarns can be closely woven. In general, the more the knots, the finer the weave, but a carpet with a thicker yarn can be expected to have fewer knots than one with a thinner yarn, so knot density is not necessarily an indication of greater quality. Don't buy a cheap, loosely knotted carpet in the fond belief that you have found a bargain. Choose something better: a carpet need not be of the very best quality to give pleasure for a hundred or more years.

In the Savonnerie carpet factory, founded in 1627, warp threads of hemp or linen were used and knot threads were cut by being wrapped in series around a cutting bar. Knotted European pile carpets were mainly made using the Turkish (symmetrical) knot.

FLAT-WEAVE TECHNIQUES

△ The most basic flat-weave technique is known as slit-weave. Where one colour stops and another starts, a vertical slit is left in the weaving.

△ There are several methods of avoiding gaps between adjacent colours. Dovetailing involves different colours returning around the same warp.

FRINGES

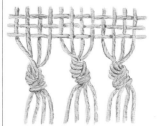

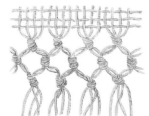

△ A simple form of fringe in which four warp threads are knotted together close to the weft to form a decorative finish.

△ This net fringe also involves knotting four warp threads together, though this time there are a series of three knots which form a net.

△ Warp threads can be looped around the end beam of the loom, rather than knotted in place. When removed, a warp-loop fringe is produced.

TUFTED RUGS

Tufting is a technique in which a tufting gun is used to insert the pile through a canvas backing. The back of the rug is coated with latex and covered with a piece of cotton cloth. Although these items are technically handmade, they are not hand-knotted and should not be sold as genuine hand-knotted rugs.

FLAT-WOVEN CARPETS

These carpets are known as kilims in Turkey or gelims in Persia and are woven in the area stretching from Anatolia to East Turkestan, and in North Africa and parts of Eastern Europe. A number of different techniques are used for flat-woven rugs, but all are based on the tapestry-weaving technique to create a flat surface with no pile. They are not woven from side to side of the work (as in all other weaving) but built up in blocks of colour. The weft threads are beaten down so hard that they completely cover the warp threads, providing solid areas of colour and very often slits, where one colour ends and another begins.

Slits are often used as part of the design in flat-woven rugs or they may be joined by various techniques such as

dovetailing the different colours round the warp threads. In most kilims, the warp threads are made of cotton and the weft threads are wool. Flat-weaving techniques have been practised by nomadic peoples, primarily to provide floor coverings, saddlecloths, sacks, blankets and cushions for use in their everyday lives. The weaving technique in itself is very simple, but there are many different qualities of weaving. It is the weaver's skill in choosing yarns, producing a close and even weave and putting together motifs to create a satisfying whole that tells in the finished product.

The dhurrie, which is the Indian version of the kilim, is usually woven in cotton rather than wool. This is a heavier rug and may be large enough to cover a whole floor, or quite small and designed to be used as a bedside rug. The weaving technique is virtually the same as in kilims. Weavers may wind the weft yarn round a bobbin to work it in and out of the warp yarns, but many prefer to work entirely by hand.

The fringes of all rugs are extensions of the warp threads, unless fake fringes are applied. The simplest fringe is formed by continuing to weave beyond the design and then cutting the rug off the loom. In this way,

VERTICAL AND HORIZONTAL LOOMS

◁△ A horizontal loom is a simple frame where the weaver moves as the work proceeds. It is easy to dismantle and transport.

▷ Vertical loom with a carpet just begun on the bottom roller. The roller-beam loom allows the warps to be unrolled from the upper beam onto the lower so that the point of work can be adjusted to suit the weaver.

the fringe is likely to unravel unless it has been tied back and sewn or finished in some other way. Fringes may be tied or knotted in various ways to prevent this from happening and to provide a decorative finish to the rug.

THE LOOM

In its most basic form, the loom for weaving pile or flat rugs is extremely simple. The nomadic or horizontal loom has hardly changed since weaving was first invented. It consists of four wooden pieces forming a rectangular frame, all fixed with pegs. This allows the loom to be dismantled without disturbing the weaving. Such looms are usually about 3ft (1m) wide, which limits the size of any woven piece.

Vertical looms, which are usually more permanent structures such as those used in village industries and urban workshops, take up less space and can be much wider than their horizontal counterparts.

MATERIALS

Wool is the yarn most commonly used for pile and flat-weave carpets, often with a cotton warp. Only in antique carpets and those woven by nomads is wool used for both the underlying foundation and for the pile. Wool is durable, good-looking and takes dyes well. It is also widely available and therefore carpets with a wool pile or weave are the most common and have the most diverse designs. Most oriental rugs are made of sheep's wool, although goat hair is sometimes found in older carpets, and in Peru, wool from the camelids (llamas and vicunas) is often used, though it does have a resistance to dyes. Many workshop rugs, made in the Middle East and China, use camel hair for the pile. The softness and sheen of old Chinese rugs comes not only from silk, but from the use of wool from baby camels.

There are several sorts of wool in Iran and the Middle East with different properties according to the breed of sheep, the climate, the height above sea level and the type of pasture. Carpets with a lustre are not necessarily more valuable than carpets that have a matt finish. The rugs and carpets made in Isfahan, for example, have little lustre but are recognized as being technically accomplished with a close, tight weave. Cotton is durable and keeps its shape, so it is particularly suitable for warp threads which act as the foundation of the whole piece. It is occasionally used to create white areas in pile carpets but, being an agricultural crop that requires settled farmers, it is not usually used by nomads and is more likely to be found in village and city workshops. Occasionally, as in the flat-woven dhurries of India, both warp and weft are cotton.

▷ The wool used to weave this bright and cheerful Turkish rug was coloured using natural vegetable dyes.

Silk has always been a luxury yarn and is not usually associated with tribal rugs. In very high quality antique carpets, silk thread was sometimes used for both warp and weft, but was usually combined with wool to make a particular area of a design stand out. These carpets are both rare and expensive. Among the most desirable are those with silk pile. They are more fragile than wool, so few old examples are to be found. Wool, cotton and silk are spun by twisting the fibres. Clockwise twisting is called Z-twisting and anti-clockwise S-twisting. Analysis of the twisting can help you to identify a carpet.

DYES AND DYEING

Dyeing the yarns for carpets is as important a process as the weaving itself. Until the 19th century, weavers dyed their own yarns using plants and other organic substances. These included saffron, henna, bark, fruit peel, nutshells, tobacco, pomegranate skins, vine leaves, tea, madder and indigo. Cochineal (a crushed insect, *Dactylopius coccus*) gave a bright red and ground-up mollusc shells could produce a shade of purple. These are usually referred to as natural dyes, although their use often required complicated, painstaking and unpleasant processes of preparation. However, the weavers understood them and used them with skill.

The first chemical dyes, introduced in the 1860s, were aniline dyes that had poor resistance to light and damaged the carpet fibres. Carpet sales suffered and the new dyes were banned in Persia in 1890. The dyers went back to natural dyes (with the exception of indigo and madder, which had to be imported and were both expensive). Early in the 20th century, aniline dyes were replaced by reliable chrome dyes, available in a wide range of colours. Some carpets show variations in the intensity or tone of a particular colour in the ground. These are caused by some fibres absorbing a dye in a different way to the rest or by the use of a batch of yarn of the same tint, but not from the same dye bath. These variations are called abrashes and can be very attractive. They are often found in tribal weaves.

PRESENT-DAY CARPET MAKERS

Most rugs and carpets are now categorized into three groups: tribal, village or workshop. Some of the most beautiful carpets in the world have been woven by the women in pastoral nomadic tribes, mainly for personal domestic purposes such as blankets, floor coverings, tent divisions and carrying bags, with any surplus being sold in local markets. Village weaving is carried out by women among settled families specifically for sale. Workshops based in cities and villages are centres of large-scale carpet production, set up to cater to the Western market.

RUGS MADE BY TRIBAL COMMUNITIES

The Quashq'ai of Iran, among the few tribes who are still truly nomadic, are typical producers of tribal-style carpets that are woven primarily for domestic use. Other producers of this type of carpet are village women who weave mainly for their homes but also sell off a proportion of their work in local markets. Nomadic tribes produce their own wool and they are still the source of wool for some of the individual village weavers.

VILLAGE RUGS

Each family may produce its own wool from its own sheep or buy woollen yarn locally. Bought-in wool may be of inferior quality, however, and it is certainly an expensive capital outlay, so these weavers often weave for contractors, who will provide the yarn and pay for the finished carpet. Village weaving for contractors has been in existence in western Turkey ever since the 17th century when rugs were produced for export to Europe. In Iran and the Caucasus, this form of weaving has certainly been in existence since the 19th century. In this sort of cottage industry, whole families or villages may undertake to weave one-off or limited edition rugs that have been designed by European or American designers.

RUGS MADE IN LARGE WORKSHOPS

Looms used by tribal women or settled villagers are seldom more than 8ft (2.4m) wide. From 1875, workshops were set up to provide larger carpets for the Western market, which became a flourishing business. Today, workshops purchase and process the raw materials, and train their employees as designers, cartoon makers, weavers, dyers, clippers and washers. This has allowed the craft to be developed to a high level and produces the uniform quality that Westerners demand. These carpets are very much geared to what is in fashion and what will sell. Workshops for large-scale production exist in Turkey, Pakistan, India, Nepal, Romania, Russia and Afghanistan. Carpet workshops have been in continuous production in China for at least 300 years.

WHERE TO BUY CARPETS

Specialist shops are often a very good source of carpets. One advantage is that you will probably get personal service from a knowledgeable salesperson and you will be allowed to take your time and discuss your purchase. You may even be allowed to take the item home and try it out for a day or two before making up your mind. Alternatively, you can buy at auction, in a department store, perhaps privately through a dealer or, for that added touch of authenticity, in the country of origin.

DEPARTMENT STORES

Some department stores have a franchised rug department, run by an independent specialist, which amounts to the same thing as a specialist shop. Many now run rug departments of their own. You will be unlikely to find anything special or unique, but you will probably find well-made, popular, good-value rugs. There may also be the advantage of an extended credit scheme.

AUCTIONS

Auctions are exciting but for the inexperienced purchaser, they can be a way to make expensive mistakes. Go armed with a list of prices of similar items seen in shops and visit a few auctions just as an observer. Find out how bidding operates and if there is a buyer's premium (probably about 10–15 per cent) on top of the bid price. Try to get a good look at the item during the viewing period before the auction. A reputable auction house will offer impartial advice but remember that attributions of age and provenance are opinions only.

PRIVATE SALES

In most countries, the buyer generally has less legal protection. If you want to buy an expensive item in this way, it would be wise to get a professional valuation. When buying from a private dealer, he or she may be able to find a particular item for you, but it is a good idea to get a reference as to his/her reliability.

BUYING IN THE COUNTRY OF ORIGIN

As a memento of your visit, buying can be interesting and satisfying, but remember that you may have to pay import tariffs and shipping costs on top of the price of the carpet. Many retail outlets (including markets) charge "tourist" prices, although bargaining may bring the price down to a reasonable sum. You may find bargaining easier in areas less popularized by tourists. In some countries, bureaucracy can make buying more of a penance than a pleasure. Always read the regulations carefully first before committing yourself to a purchase.

CHOOSING THE RIGHT CARPET

Faded colours do not necessarily mean that a carpet is old: chemical washing can fade the colours very quickly. Attributing rugs to a place or time can be very difficult. Prices fluctuate depending on many factors, including exchange rates and import tariffs in different countries and availability. Rugs are more likely to be priced on individual merit than on size. Comparing items from different weaving regions is difficult too, because of the variations in local production costs. In short, when buying a carpet, it really is best to rely on the individual merit of the rug in question and on personal taste and budget.

BUYING NEW CARPETS

The first rule when buying a new carpet is: look for something that you really like and don't waste any time looking for a bargain or imagining you can necessarily use it as an investment. When buying a hand-knotted or flat-woven rug, always look at the back of it. The pattern should be just as clear there as on the front of the rug. In machine-made carpets and rugs, the threads at the back may overlap and look muddled. Check that the pile is knotted in: if you pull a thread, it should not come away. Pull the fringe (gently) at each end of the carpet. This should be made of the extreme ends of the warp threads and it should be an integral part of the carpet and not added later on.

Important considerations to bear in mind are the aesthetic qualities of the carpet – its combination of patterns, colours and yarns and the technical quality of the weaving – how closely the carpet has been woven, the nature of the wool and dyes used and its age and general condition. Always look at the back of the carpet because the number of knots varies enormously between different types and qualities from, say, 40 knots up to about 500 or more per 4in (10cm) square. However, some quite outstanding carpets may have only 50 knots per 4in (10cm) while others will be very run of the mill, even if they have 150 knots to the 4in (10cm) square.

BUYING OLD CARPETS

In general, old carpets are more valuable than new ones. From the 19th century onwards, carpets were woven more and more to meet Western tastes and although these are still of great interest and value, they have lost much of the individuality of the earlier examples. Antique carpets are very likely to have been repaired over the years. If skilfully done, they should have declined little in value. However, if the work has been badly done or is too obvious, then the value of the carpet will almost certainly have fallen. Any carpet will be worn to some extent after 50 years or so. If it is evenly worn over the whole surface, the carpet will still be considered good. If

△ Always look at the back of a carpet to see how tightly woven it is. This is a good quality carpet with fine, even knotting.

△ This carpet has an obvious worn patch and should not be bought as an investment or placed in a heavy traffic area.

it has been very worn in patches, then it will have lost a great deal of value and will also be difficult to repair.

Establishing the date of a carpet can be very difficult. Dates in Islamic numbers or translated into Western dates and characters may appear in the border or field of a carpet. These are not always reliable and may even have been added by a weaver to increase a carpet's value. Carpet styles and motifs do not help much because the same designs have been used in every production area for centuries. The state of preservation should be considered, but is not always a reliable factor. Establishing whether chemical dyes have been used may date a carpet as being manufactured later than 1860–1870. Antique carpets usually have well balanced designs including the use of open and filled spaces, whereas recent examples are often more haphazard. Older carpets are likely to have traditional motifs that have been woven and incorporated in traditional ways, while newer ones may use the same motifs but in a more stylized and exaggerated form. Colour is important too. The oldest carpets usually have many strong, brilliant colours, while those from the 20th century generally use fewer colours in more pastel tones.

If you are new to carpets and are thinking of buying something valuable, do get professional advice – at least until you have learned how to recognize what to look for in quality and where potential problems may lie.

SIZE

When shopping, never go anywhere without a tape measure: a rug that is too large for the space allotted to it will suffer. If it rubs against a wall, the edges will eventually fray; if you have to fold it back, the yarn will become damaged and the rug will become worn along the folded section. Besides that, it will not look good, because it will not be seen as a complete piece. A rug that is too small, on the other hand, will look diminished. If you want a rug under a dining table, for example, and it only just fits under the legs, it will lose much of its dignity and the full effect of its marvellous patterns and colours will be lost.

HOW TO SPOT PROBLEMS

A repaired carpet will be less valuable than a perfect one. Much will depend on the quality of the repair. Some repairers are so skilful at matching colours and wools that the mended parts are practically invisible. Sometimes new knots are inserted to re-pile worn parts. Very small areas of re-piling are acceptable, but most experts would agree that it is better to conserve what is already there rather than to try to reproduce it with the wrong wool and the wrong dyes, which will fade differently. Inspect the whole carpet carefully. All sorts of problems can lie hidden inside a rolled-up carpet including moth damage, holes, badly repaired patches and rot.

ALTERATIONS AND CUTS

Carpets are often shortened or reduced in width so that they fit into a particular space. Sometimes this has been done so skilfully that only an expert would realize, but a cut carpet will have a reduced value.

PATCHES

If a patch has been glued onto a carpet at the back, be wary. You can remove anything glued with animal glue, but rubber-based glues will ruin a carpet.

ROT

A carpet that has been saturated in water for any length of time will become brittle and small cracks or splits may be seen on the back.

STAINS

Don't buy stained carpets. It will be impossible to tell what has caused the stain and it may be impossible to remove it. This will reduce the value of the carpet and it does not look good.

WORN PATCHES

In a pile carpet, the pile will be gone and the warp threads may be visible. Check that the white warp threads have not been camouflaged with paint.

MOTH-EATEN PATCHES

Study the back of the carpet for tell-tale holes in the warp threads. Carpets with a lot of moth damage are usually not worth buying, though a few small holes are easily repaired.

BORDERS AND FRINGES

You may find that the carpet fringes have been vacuumed to a frazzle. Carpets are often repaired by removing the pile back to a convenient line and fraying out the ends into a new fringe – or the outer border may be missing altogether. Missing borders can reduce a carpet's value substantially.

TINTING

A cheap way to bring back original colour to a worn carpet is to tint the worn part to match the surrounding pile. Retouching with leather dyes, waterproof inks or felt-tip pens is known as painting in the trade and greatly reduces the value of a carpet.

COLOUR

Although it is true that nearly all rugs will fit into almost any interior scheme, there is great satisfaction in finding one that fits into your own scheme as though it were made for it. To a certain extent, this is to do with personal taste. If you know your own tastes in terms of the home in general, the carpet or rug you are drawn to will probably fit in. But don't hurry your choice. Most specialist companies understand the importance of choosing a carpet carefully and will be happy to let you spend as much time as you like sorting through and examining what they have in stock. Many shops will allow you to take a rug home and try it out *in situ* for a

△ Sunshine glancing through the window highlights the golden wood of the furniture and the rich red of the rug.

SUITABLE BACKGROUNDS FOR CARPETS AND RUGS

When choosing your carpet, always bear in mind the area in which the carpet will be placed. For example, some colours and patterns will look great on a background of marble; others will look dreadful. There is a huge range of floor coverings available that make perfect settings for beautiful carpets and rugs.

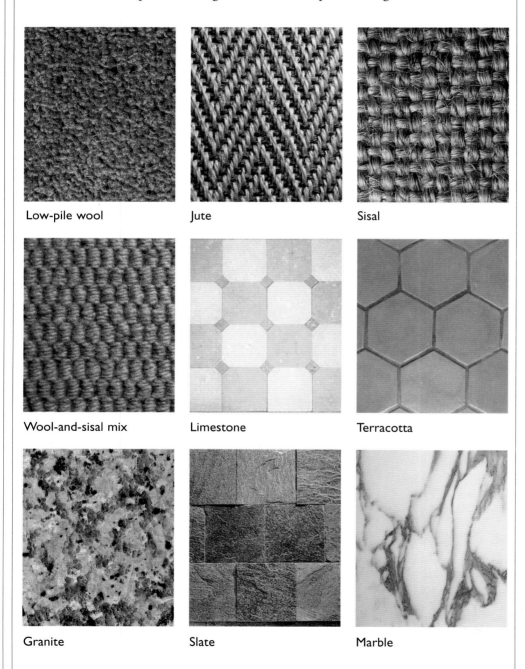

Low-pile wool

Jute

Sisal

Wool-and-sisal mix

Limestone

Terracotta

Granite

Slate

Marble

△ An underlay such as this will prevent rugs from slipping around the floor, which can be extremely dangerous.

day or two. Rugs are woven with enormous care and centuries of skill – recognizing and choosing those you like should not be hurried either.

FITNESS FOR PURPOSE

Rugs are, by nature, durable and tough and many of the most beautiful carpets are made to withstand the patter of feet for many years. However, it would be less than sensible to put a fine pile carpet in an entrance hall where heavy boots will be treading mud into it, day in and day out, and where poor lighting will mean that its beauty is neither seen nor appreciated. Antique carpets should be placed with care and may be better hung on the wall, where their colours and designs may be appreciated face-to-face, so to speak. Always place rugs on a carpeted floor or underlay to protect them as they are heavy and solid. Solid sponge rubber is best (not foam or ripple rubber) or a natural floor covering, such as jute or coir coated with rubber on one side. Choosing a rug that is suitable for the space in which you intend to place it and taking care of how it is placed will be well worth the effort.

LOOKING AFTER YOUR CARPETS

If you look after your carpet well, it should remain as attractive as when you first bought it. Advice is given throughout the Style Directory about each carpet style's durability and suitability for certain areas in the home, and there are a few basic principles which should always be applied. Do not place houseplants on a rug as the humidity needed by the plants often causes mildew, and avoid placing a rug in full sunlight as the colours will fade. Otherwise, occasional careful cleaning should be all you need to do. If problems do arise, seek the advice of a professional.

REPAIRS

Repairs should always be carried out by professionals, particularly on antique or expensive rugs. Partially detached fringes or selvedges can be resewn by hand using matching-coloured wool or silk, but damage to the pile or foundation should always be handled by a specialist. A local specialist shop or one of the larger auction houses should be able to give you the address of a reliable cleaner/repairer.

If the rug starts curling at the edges (which may happen in tightly knotted rugs), sew a PVC or fabric strip along the sides, taking care that it is invisible from the surface of the rug. Never use glue for this as it will make the carpet brittle and may stain it.

◁ This carpet has been repaired so you can hardly notice where it was damaged. Colours and pattern have been matched very precisely and the repair will be durable.

◁ This carpet has been poorly repaired: the repair is easily noticeable with stitches showing and the repaired area will be weak.

REPAIRING A FLAT-WEAVE

▷ The damaged area is laid out flat on a table.

▷▷ A woollen thread is run all around the damaged area, about ½in (1cm) into the undamaged area.

▷ Threads are run backwards and forwards, to take the place of the damaged warp threads.

▷▷ The threads are taken right into the undamaged part of the carpet to give them long-term strength.

▷ Carefully matched woollen threads are meticulously darned into the warp threads.

▷▷ The darning is carried over the whole of the damaged area.

PROTECTING AN EDGE

▷ Special fabric strips are sewn along the sides of the rug to prevent it from curling at the edges. This will also help to stop the rug slipping, which can be dangerous.

MENDING AN EDGE

▷ The theads that have become separated are individually and meticulously bound with matching thread. Any threads showing when the work is completed are clipped.

CREATING A FRINGE

▷ Natural coloured wool is looped through the weft threads of the carpet and secured where they will be hidden by the pile. The threads are then trimmed evenly.

If a kilim begins to come apart at the slits within the design or the edges, it is better (and not difficult) to sew it with matching cotton or wool thread, rather than to let the damage grow worse. Never try to do this yourself with a valuable kilim, of course.

CLEANING

Both dust and grit can cause great damage so carpets that are often walked on should be cleaned regularly using a carpet sweeper or vacuum cleaner without a beater. If a beater is used, it may damage the carpet. Run the cleaner's head gently and slowly over the carpet. Pressure (or rubbing) will damage the fibres. Shake the rug gently to dislodge more dust. Fragile carpets should not be walked on and should be vacuumed only once or twice a year using a special dusting cleaner with nylon net fixed over the opening. Carpet fringes are particularly vulnerable when cleaning so take care that they do not become caught up. Do not attempt any washing or dry cleaning without consulting an expert, and always have the carpet cleaned and shampooed if you are going to put it into store. Never cover a carpet with polythene sheeting when storing as this will make it sweat. Instead, cover both sides with acid-free tissue paper and roll it carefully in the direction of the nap over a pole, such as plastic drainpipe. Finally, wrap it in cloth, for example an old sheet, which has been treated with mothproofing.

INSURANCE

Insurance against damage and theft is always advisable. Most items can be included in the general household policy, but separate cover is recommended for more expensive carpets. Keep photographs and descriptions of these and get a valuation when you buy the carpet, or have it valued once you have brought it home. Remember that the insurance or valuation is not necessarily what you paid for the carpet, but what you would pay for a replacement, which may be a larger sum. Have your carpet reassessed regularly for insurance purposes, as the value can change significantly over time.

Glossary

Abrash
Variations of density in a color, seen in a carpet by irregular horizontal washes; caused by the wool being dyed at different times in different batches of color, which is of unequal density. Although an accidental and therefore arbitrary process, abrash can greatly enhance the beauty of a carpet.

Aniline
Chemical dye, a derivative of coal-tar. First produced in the 1860's and ubiquitous in the Middle East from the 1880's. Most frequently encountered in the red–blue–purple range, the substance being named after *anil*, the indigo plant. Colors are very fugitive; a bright orange-pink, for instance, will fade at the tip to walnut-brown.

Boteh
Widespread pattern of Persian origin (Persian for cluster of leaves). Resembles a pear or pine cone, by which names it has been known in the West. Symbolic connections have also been suggested, somewhat fancifully, between it and the Flame of Zoroastra, the imprint of a fist on wet plaster, the loop in the river Jumna, etc. Best known in Europe as the principal motif of the paisley pattern.

Chinese fret
Pattern of interlocking swastikas. Sometimes called the *wan* pattern, wan being the Chinese character representing 10,000 (i.e. a swastika).

Chrome dye
A fast synthetic dye mordanted with potassium bichromate. This, and other more recent synthetic colors, are now used in all the major rug weaving areas of the world. Although fast, the colors are harsh and dead.

Cloudband
Cloud motif used in Anatolia, Central Asia, Persia, and China. May be featured individually, or interlinked to form a meandering border.

Cochineal
Scarlet red similar to but more brilliant than lac. Obtained from the crushed bodies of a female insect native to Mexico and the West Indies, and imported into Europe from the 16th century (not into the Middle East until the end of the 18th century). Supposed until the 18th century to be the berry or seed of an oak.

Compound-weave
Technical term for pieces made with more than one set of either warp or weft elements, or both. A form of flat-weaving.

Dhurrie
Indian and Pakistani flat-weave, similar in technique and look to a kilim, but made of cotton rather than wool.

Flat-weave
Any carpet, rug, or other textile woven without a pile. Kilims, soumaks, dhurries, and vernehs are all flat-weaves.

Gul
A lozenge-shaped motif, usually arranged in vertical rows. It is actually a stylized flower head (gul is Persian for flower). There are numerous different types of gul.

Herati
Also called the *mahi* or fish pattern. As its name implies, this floral pattern is supposed to have originated in east Persia. Consists of a repeat of a flower head, bracketed by two serrated-edged lanceolate leaves. This is probably the most frequently used of all oriental floral designs.

Indigo
Blue dye obtained from the leaves of the indigo plant, one of the various species of *Indigofera*, a tropical genus of *Papilionaceae*. Native to India, from whence most of the leaves used in the preparation of the dye in Persia were exported. The dye was prepared from the fermented compound of crushed indigo leaves, red clay slip. potash, grape sugar, and slaked lime.

Jufti
"False" knot, either Turkish or Persian, whereby the knots are tied to four, not two, warp threads, thus coarsening the weave and halving the time involved in production. Became prevalent in Persia in the late 19th century, although for a time it was officially banned.

Kilim
Also spelled kelim, khilim, kileem, gilim, ghilim, gelim, dilim, etc. Form of flat-weaving associated principally with Anatolia.

Kermes
Crushed body of a female inset that gives a red similar to cochineal and lac. The insect breeds on the Kermes oak (*Quercus coccifera*). Its use in carpets has never been satisfactorily established.

Knotted-pile carpets
Made with short lengths of yarn (usually wool, but sometimes silk) that are looped or knotted around the warp threads on the loom to form a pile, which stands at right angles to the warp.

Lac
Also laq, meaning literally "hundreds of thousands." Name given to a brilliant deep purple-red obtained from melting and straining the resinous excretions of the *Tachardia lacca*, a scale insect native to India that covers the twigs of certain trees in a resinous substance for the purpose of immuring the female of the species. The red dye, like that of cochineal and kermes, is the extract of the female bodies of the insect, which in this case are gathered with the resin.

Lampas
A method of weaving so that the pattern is raised in relief against the ground. This technique is a form of embroidery.

Loom
A structure of four wooden pieces forming a rectangular frame. Designed to hold the warp threads under tension while the wefts are woven in place, or the pile yarn knotted. Can be horizontal or vertical, permanent or temporary.

Madder
Deep red-brown dye extracted from the root of the *Rubia tinctorum* or other Rubia plants.

Medallion
A dominant motif that forms the main design element of a carpet. They can either be used individually in the center of the rug, or several may be used across the piece. The latter have an heraldic quality and are known as amulets.

Mina khani
Floral pattern said to have been named after Mina Khan, although this is certainly apocryphal. Repeat pattern of large palmettes and small white flowers contained in a lattice of stems. Stylized geometrical versions are found in certain tribal carpets, such as those of the Belouch.

Mordant
A chemical substance with which the wool is treated in order to fix the dye color. It can itself affect the eventual color of the carpet and can be corrosive.

Palas
Caucasian name for a flat-weave.

Palmette
A flower head of heart-shape with many radiating lobes or petals.

Pomegranate ring
Gives a dull yellow dye.

Quatrefoil
Medallion with four rounded lobe sections.

Sarköy
Also sharkyoy. Name for kilims made in Thrace.

Saph
Prayer rug with multiple mihrabs (niches).

Selvedge
The outer warps of the rug on the long sides, which are overcast to form firm braided edges. On many tribal pieces, these are further strengthened with goat's hair.

Shou and fu
Motifs symbolizing long life and good luck. Most symbolic Chinese characters are referred to as shou or fu, regardless of their form.

Soumak
Also sumak, summak, sumacq, and sumakh. Thought to be a corruption of Shemajka, a town in southeast Caucasus. Technique of progressive weft wrapping.

Spandrel
Architectural term for the space between the curve of an arch and the enclosing moldings. Thus the space immediately above the arch of the mihrab in a prayer rug.

Swastika
A hooked cross. Chinese symbol for 10,000 (*wan*) and happiness. In many cultures, a symbol of the sun. An extraordinarily ubiquitous symbol, found contemporaneously as far apart as pre-Columbian America and China. The swastika appears in the work of almost all known cultures around the world.

Tree-of-life
An ancient religious symbol predating both Islam and Christianity. It represents the connection between this world and paradise.

Verneh
Also verné. Thought to a corruption of a now unknown Caucasian place name. Technically, these pieces are either soumak or brocaded rugs (or sometimes a mixture); stylistically, the name usually applies to pieces woven with a design of squares, containing either geometric motifs, or a mixture of geometric and animals motifs.

Vine leaves
Give a yellow dye.

Warp
Longitudinal threads forming part of the foundation of a carpet.

Weft
Latitudinal threads forming part of the foundation of a carpet.

Weld
Extract of the *Reselda lutuola* plant. Gives a yellow dye.

Whey
Watery part of milk, used in combination with madder, to give a rose red that is found on certain Sultanabad carpets.

SUPPLIERS

CANADA

EL PIPIL CRAFTS
267 Danforth Avenue
Toronto
Ontario M4K 1N2
Tel: 416 465 9625

THE ORIENTAL CARPET STORE
55 York Street
Stratford
Ontario N5A 1A1
Tel: 519 273 3207

VERNACULAR
1166 Yonge Street
Toronto
Ontario M4W 2L9
Tel: 416 961 6490

THE WHEAT SHEAF
R. R. 2
Milford
Ontario K0K 2PO
Tel: 613 476 7730

WOVEN GARDENS
816 Rue Ouimet
P. O. Box 1769
St Jovite
Quebec J0T 2HO
Tel: 819 425 8491

UNITED STATES

ABC CARPET & HOME
888 Broadway
New York
NY 10003
Tel: 212 473 3000

ABSOLUTELY RUGS!
7301 North Federal Highway
Boca Raton
FL 33487
Tel: 407 997 1688

ADRASKAND
15 Ross Avenue
San Anselmo
CA 94960
Tel: 415 459 1711

ANAHITA GALLERY
P. O. Box 1305
Santa Monica
CA 90406
Tel: 213 455 2310

ANTIQUE CARPET GALLERY
533 S. E. Grand Avenue
Portland
OR 97214
Tel: 503 234 1345

ARIANA RUG GALLERY
411 King Street
Alexandria
VA 22314
Tel: 703 683 3206

ASIA MINOR CARPETS
801 Lexington Avenue
New York
NY 10021
Tel: 212 223 2288

J. R. AZIZOLLAHOFF
303 Fifth Avenue Suite 701
New York
NY 10016
Tel: 212 689 5396

BEBERE IMPORTS
144 South Robertson
  Boulevard
Los Angeles
CA 90048
Tel: 213 274 7064

JAMES BLACKMON GALLERY
2140 Bush Street #1
San Francisco
CA 94115
Tel: 415 922 1859

CASA DOS TAPETES DE ARRAIOLOS
D&D Building
979 Third Avenue
New York
NY 10022
Tel: 212 688 9330

DENNIS R. DODDS/MAQAM
19 West 55th Street
Suite 6A
New York
NY 10019
Tel: 212 977 3603

FOOTHILL ORIENTAL RUGS
1464 Foothill Drive
Salt Lake City
UT 84108
Tel: 801 582 3500

F. J. HAKIMIAN
136 East 57th Street
Suite 201
New York
NY 1002-2707
Tel: 212 371 6900

KRIKOR MARKARIAN
151 West 30th Street

Room 801
New York
NY 10001
Tel: 212 629 8683

MOMEMI
36 East Street
2nd Floor
New York
NY 10016
Tel: 212 532 9577

MSM INDUSTRIES
802 Swan Drive
P. O. Box 707
Smyrna
TN 37167
Tel: 615 355 4355

STEPHEN A. MILLER ORIENTAL RUGS
212 Galisteo Street
Santa F
NM 87501
Tel: 505 983 8231

NOMAD
279 Newbury Street
Boston
MA 02116
Tel: 617 267 9677

NOURISON
100 Park Plaza Drive
Secaucus
NJ 07094
Tel: 201 867 6900

O'BANNON ORIENTAL CARPETS
5666 Northumberland
  Street
Pittsburgh
PA 15217
Tel: 412 422 0300

OBATU-AFSHAR
311 West Superior
Suite 309
Chicago
IL 60610
Tel: 312 943 1189

JAMES OPIE ORIENTAL RUGS
214 SW Stark Street
Portland
Oregon
OR 97204
Tel: 503 226 0116

THE PILLOWRY L. A.
8687 Melrose Avenue
G770 West Hollywood
CA 90069
and
132 East 61st Street
New York
NY 10021
Tel: 212 308 1630

THE RUG COLLECTOR'S GALLERY
2460 Fairmont Boulevard
Cleveland Heights
OH 44106
Tel: 216 721 9333

SANDERS AND COMPANY
270 Madison Avenue
Suite 1300
New York
NY 10016
Tel: 212 685 1745

SHAVER RAMSAY ORIENTAL GALLERIES
2414 East Third Avenue
Denver
CO 80206
Tel: 303 320 6363

MARK SHILEN GALLERY
109 Green Street
New York
NY 10012
Tel: 212 925 3394

SILK ROUTE CORP
3119 Fillmore Street
San Francisco
CA 94123
Tel: 415 563 4936

SKINNER
The Heritage On the
  Garden
63 Park Plaza
Boston
MA 02116
and
357 Main Street
Bolton
MA 01740
Tel: 508 779 6241

LE SOUK GALLERY
1001 East Alameda
Santa Fe
NM 87501
Tel: 505 989 8765

STARK CARPET CORPORATION
979 Third Avenue
New York
NY 10022-1276
Tel: 212 752 9000

SUN BOW TRADING CO.
108 Fourth Street NE
Charlottesville
VA 22901
Tel: 804 293 8821

TAMOR SHAH
3219 Cains Hill Place NE
Atlanta

GA 30305
Tel: 404 261 7259

TROCADERO TEXTILE & NOMADIC ART
2313 Calvert Street
Conneticut Avenue NW
Washington
DC 20008
Tel: 202 328 8440

WOVEN LEGENDS
4700 Wissahickon Avenue
#106
Philadelphia
PA 19144
Tel: 215 849 8344

UNITED KINGDOM

AARON GALLERY
34 Bruton Street
London W1X 7DD
Tel: 0171 499 9434/5

AXMINSTER CARPETS
Axminster
Devon EX13 5PQ
Tel: 01297 32244

CHANDNI CHOWK
1 Harlequins, Paul Street
Exeter EX4 3TT
Tel: 01392 410 201

COATS
4 Kensington Church Walk
London W8 4NB
Tel: 0171 937 0983

COUNTRY & EASTERN
3 Holland Street
Kensington
London W8
Tel: 0171 938 2711

EASTERN ARTIFACTS
42-3 Royal Park Terrace
Edinburgh EH8 8JA
Tel: 0131 652 1962

EGE CARPETS
Ege House
Drumhead Road
Chorley North Business Park
Chorley PR6 7BZ
Tel: 01257 293000

FAIRMAN GALLERY
218 Westbourne Road
London W11 2RH
Tel: 0171 229 2262

CHRISTOPHER FARR
115 Regents Park Walk
Primrose Hill
London NW1 8UR
Tel: 0171 916 7690

JOSS GRAHAM
10 Eccleston Street
London SW1W 9LT
Tel: 0171 730 4370

HABITAT
The Heal's Building
196 Tottenham Court Road
London W1P 9LD
Tel: 0171 255 2545

J. P. J. HOMER
Stoneleigh
Parabola Road
Cheltenham GL50 3BD
Tel: 01242 2234 243

ALASTAIR HULL
18A High Street
Haddenham
Ely
Cambridge CB6 3TA
Tel: 01353 740 577

KESHISHIAN
73 Pimlico Road
London SW1
Tel: 0171 730 8810

CHRISTOPHER LEGGE
25 Oakthorpe Road
Summertown
Oxford OX2 7BD
Tel: 01865 57572

LIBERTY
Regent Street
London W1R 6AH
Tel: 0171 734 1234

MANSOUR
56 South Audley Street
London W1Y 5FA
Tel: 0171 499 5601

MARTIN & FROST
130 McDonald Road
Edinburgh EH7 4HN
Tel: 0131 557 8787

MOROCCAN RUGS & WEAVINGS
5A Calabria Road
London N5 1JB
Tel: 0171 226 7908

GARRY MUSE
26 Mostyn Gardens
London NW10
Tel: 0181 969 5460

ORIENTAL RUG GALLERY
15-6 High Street
Eton
Berkshire
Tel: 01753 623 000

ORIENTAL RUGS OF BATH
17 Argyle Street

Bath BA2 4BQ
Tel: 01225 465558

ORIENTIS
Digby Road
Sherborne
Dorset DT9 3NL
Tel: 01935 816 479/
813 274

OUT OF THE NOMAD'S TENT
21 St Leonards Lane
Edinburgh EH8 9SH
Tel: 0131 662 1612

THE PERSIAN CARPET STUDIO
Harrow Street
Leavenheath
Colchester CO6 4PN
Tel: 01787 210034

THE TEXTILE GALLERY
12 Queen Street
Mayfair
London W1X 7PL
Tel: 0171 499 7979

TUMI
8/9 New Bond Street Place
Bath BA1 1BH
Tel: 01225 462367

DENNIS WOODMAN
105 North Road
Kew
Surrey TW9 4HJ
Tel: 0181 878 8182

ALEX ZADAH
35 Bruton Place
London W1X 7AB
Tel: 0171 493 2622/
2673

INDEX

Page numbers in *italics* refer to captions

CREDITS

ABC Carpet & Home p.41(tl), p.55, p.81, p.144

Berengar Antiques p.22, p.30(r), p.36, p.149

Crowson Fabrics p.29

Egetaepper (UK) Ltd p.31, p.34, p.134(tl), p.135(r)

Christopher Farr Handmade Rugs p.11(r), p.127(c), p.132, p.133(tl&r), p.134(bl, tr& br), p.135(tl&bl), p.136(tl&tr), p.137(tr&br)

Fairman Ltd p.44(r), p.45(bl), p.47(l), p.47(b), p.56(l), p.96(r), p.97(b), p.99(tr), p.100, p.101(b), p.102, p.103, p.133(bl&r)

Fired Earth p.21, p.24/25, p.26(t), p.27, p.30(l), p.37(t)

Gallery Zadah p.14(l&c), p.15(l), p.44(l), p.45(br), p.57(bl), p.60, p.61(br), p.64, p.65(br), p.67(tl&bl), p.69(tr, bl&br), p.70, p.71, p.78(tl&tr), p.79(l), p.87(bl), p.97(t), p.98(tl&bl), p.101(tl&tr), p.111(tl&r), p.129(bl&tr)

Raija Grahn p.108(l&r)

Habitat p.18/19, p.23, p.28(l), p.35

F.J. Hakimian Inc p.8(r), p.9(r), p.10, p.11(l), p.14(r), p.41(tr&br), p.46, p.47(tr), p.50(tl), p.51(bl&tr), p.75(bl), p.83(bl), p.86(c), p.87(tr), p.107(tr), p.109, p.112, p.113, p.114, p.115, p.116

Hali Publications Ltd p.15(r), p.53(tr&br), p.63, p.65(tl, tr&bc), p.68(r), p.69(tl), p.73, p.74, p.75(tl&tr), p.76, p.77, p.79, p.82(b), p.85(t), p.93(r)

Heriatge Bathrooms PLC p.32(t)

Ikea Ltd p.37(b)

Keshishian p.13(l), p.41(bl), p.43, p.45(tr), p.48(r), p.49(t&b), p.50(tr&br), p.51(tl), p.52, p.53(tl&bl), p.56(r), p.57(br), p.82(t), p.87(tl), p.105, p.106(t), p.107(tl&bl), p.110, p.111(b), p.128, p.129(tl&br), p.130, p.131

Liberty Ltd p.6(tl), p.9(l), p.13(r), p.40

Momeni Inc. p.121

MSM Industries p.150(tr)

Martin Norris p.151, p.152, p.153

Out Of The Nomads p.61(bl), p.84(l), p.106(b)

Barty Phillips p.136(tc), p.137(tl&bl)

Skinner, Inc. p.119, p.122, p.123

Thanakra p.90, p.91, p.92, p.93(l)

Tumi Ltd p.124, p.125

Wood Bros Furniture Ltd p.18(l), p.33

Azeri® Folklife Carpet, Woven Legends® Inc./Gary McKinnis p.59(tl)

Black Mountain Looms®, Woven Legends® Inc./Henry Glassie, George Jevremovic, Gary McKinnis, Teddy Summer p.12(bl), p.59(tr), p.59(br&bl), p.83(t&bl), p.85(bl&br), p.140(b), p.141, p.146(b)

Les Wies p.1, p.2, p.3, p.4, p.5, p.16, p.17, p.38, p.39, p.138, p.139

Zee Stone Gallery p.8(l), p.12(tl), p.95, p.98(r), p.99(tl&b).